THE RIGHTS OF GROUPS

The Rights of Groups

*Understanding Community
in the Eyes of the Law*

Lawrence Rosen

NEW YORK UNIVERSITY PRESS

New York

NEW YORK UNIVERSITY PRESS
New York
www.nyupress.org

References to Internet websites (URLs) were accurate at the time of writing. Neither the author nor New York University Press is responsible for URLs that may have expired or changed since the manuscript was prepared.

Library of Congress Cataloging-in-Publication Data
Names: Rosen, Lawrence, 1941–   author.
Title: The rights of groups : understanding community in the eyes of the law / Lawrence Rosen.
Description: New York : New York University Press, 2024. | Includes bibliographical references and index. | Summary: "Viewed through the lens of cultural theory, the concept of community that is vital to Americans' self-image is explored in a number of social and legal contexts, including recent decisions about abortion, Native rights, university investments, and the ownership of cultural property"—Provided by publisher.
Identifiers: LCCN 2023038547 (print) | LCCN 2023038548 (ebook) | ISBN 9781479830411 (hardback) | ISBN 9781479830442 (ebook) | ISBN 9781479830459 (ebook other)
Subjects: LCSH: Group rights. | Group rights—United States. | Indigenous peoples—Legal status, laws, etc.—United States. | Libel and slander—United States. | United States. Supreme Court.
Classification: LCC K3240 .R693 2024 (print) | LCC K3240 (ebook) | DDC342.7308/7—dc23/eng/20231003
LC record available at https://lccn.loc.gov/2023038547
LC ebook record available at https://lccn.loc.gov/2023038548

New York University Press books are printed on acid-free paper, and their binding materials are chosen for strength and durability. We strive to use environmentally responsible suppliers and materials to the greatest extent possible in publishing our books.

Manufactured in the United States of America

10 9 8 7 6 5 4 3 2 1

Also available as an ebook

For Kaya Malika and Miriam

CONTENTS

Introduction

The American Romance of Community

Americans are in love with the idea of community. Barack Obama was lauded as a "community organizer," *Reader's Digest* urges each of us to "find your community," and even murderous spies congratulate themselves as members of the "intelligence community." Such references, however idealized, point to a deep ambivalence in the institutions that support the place of community among the categories of civic and legal organization. The constitutional structure of the United States divides power between the central authority (state or federal) and the individual, leaving no formal space for the collectivity. Admittedly, the contradiction between the idealization and the legal reality does, on occasion, yield a strained recognition of some intermediate entity: The Amish may be said to risk destruction as a community if their children are required to attend school beyond the eighth grade, while some ethnic groups have successfully contested urban plans that would sever their neighborhood. But overall the romance of community and the reality of its everyday life constitute a dilemma that challenges both our vision of ourselves and the terms by which we render that vision palpable.

We are, then, faced with something of a predicament: while the individual and the community need hardly be in contradiction, their interests do not necessarily and at all times coincide. Nor does a clear concept of the place of a community within the legal scheme leap out from our constitutional structure or from generations of case law. Understanding and coping with this apparent incongruity has a long history in American politics and letters. In the process of unpacking the complex relation of community to the broader culture we may need to consider a bit about its intellectual history. And for that purpose no better guide exists than that most astute of early American visitors, Alexis de Tocqueville.

When Tocqueville wrote *Democracy in America* he used the recently coined term "individualism" to refer to the social and political climate that conduces each member of the polity to concentrate on his or her small sphere of well-being to the detriment of any broader societal commitment. "Individualism," he wrote, "is not the same as 'egoism'—a passionate and exaggerated love of self which leads a man to think of all things in terms of himself and to prefer himself to all"—but is, instead, "a calm and considered feeling which disposes each citizen to isolate himself from the mass of his fellows and withdraw into the circle of family and friends; with this little society formed to his taste, he gladly leaves the greater society to look after itself."[1] Tocqueville feared that "democratic man" would always be a separated creature, disconnected from a set of relationships of the sort that were at least provided by an aristocratic order: "Thus not only does democracy make each man forget his ancestors, but it hides his descendants from him and separates him from his contemporaries; it constantly leads him back towards himself alone and threatens finally to confine him wholly in the solitude of his own heart."[2] While admiring the American sense of egalitarianism, Tocqueville found himself stressing the downside: "Equality," he concluded, "puts men side by side without a common link to hold them firm."[3]

To counter this tendency, Tocqueville believed, the Founders wisely created numerous structures of government that, by drawing together personal and collective interests, would have the effect of producing a feeling of interdependence. Yet the danger would remain that since individualism is itself both a product and an exemplar of social equality—and might expand as democracy renders society increasingly egalitarian—the willingness to abandon the forum of local government and the ideology of political liberty might prove overpowering. It is this threat—that each person "may be shut up in the solitude of his own heart"—that seemed to threaten any hope for a sense of community not coincident with the family or the state.

And yet, even for Tocqueville, alternatives to rampant individualism were discernible. Two factors were especially noteworthy for him in this regard. The first was that family, however bounded and distinctive for each person, took people out of their individual selves and cast them into a circle of common concern. What happens in America, he claimed, is that "[d]emocracy loosens social bonds, but it tightens natural bonds."

Second, he noted the extraordinary tendency of Americans to group themselves in a wide range of (often temporary and purpose-driven) voluntary associations:

> As soon as several of the inhabitants of the United States have conceived a sentiment or an idea that they want to produce in the world, they seek each other out; and when they have found each other, they unite. From then on, they are no longer isolated men, but a power one sees from afar, whose actions serve as an example; a power that speaks, and to which one listens. . . . There is nothing, in my view, that deserves more to attract our regard than the intellectual and moral associations of America.[4]

This does not mean that there is an absence of attachment to the nation as a whole. To the contrary:

> It would be unjust to believe that the patriotism of the American and the zeal that each of them shows for the well-being of his fellow citizens have nothing real about them. Although private interest directs most human actions, in the United States as elsewhere, it does not rule all.
>
> I must say that I often see Americans make great and genuine sacrifices for the public, and I remarked a hundred times that, when needed, they almost never fail to lend faithful support to one another. . . . [T]here is scarcely an undertaking so small that Americans do not unite for it.[5]

Tocqueville's emphasis on the ways in which Americans counter their isolation through participation in voluntary associations is at once a recognition of community and a particular version of it. Indeed, these attachments are not without an emotional valence not unlike that felt if one believes that God has assigned individuals their proper place in the social order. "Sentiments and ideas," he writes, "renew themselves, the heart is enlarged, and the human mind is developed only by the reciprocal action of men upon one another. I have shown that this action is almost nonexistent in a democratic country. It is therefore necessary to create it artificially there. And this is what associations alone can do."[6]

Each voluntary grouping is thus created and maintained by its members but does not necessarily have the legacy or staying power of those relationships based on social hierarchy, class, or genealogy that, he argued, sustain the structure of a society. Tocqueville may seem to have it both ways when he says that, for an individual American, democracy "constantly leads him back to himself alone" while simultaneously noting that "Americans of all ages, all conditions, all minds constantly unite," that "they seek each other out," and that "[i]n democratic countries the science of association is the mother science, and progress of all the others depends on the progress of that one." Close family ties and voluntary associations thus lack the enduring attachments found in aristocratic cultures and for which alternative associations may be a poor substitute. As he notes: "Democracy brings relatives together at the same time that it separates citizens."[7] Given such categories, it may seem inevitable that later Americans should focus on groupings that can be analogized to corporations while in the law corporations should be seen as persons.

"Community" in the American context may, then, be both an open-textured concept and one that preserves a claim on the nation's sentiment and self-image. In the years since Tocqueville wrote, the concept of community has been subject to numerous interpretations and uses. In his seminal book *The Lonely Crowd*, David Riesman, for example, argued that American political institutions are too amorphous and fickle to garner the emotional equivalent of attachment to a sense of real community, while Robert Bellah and his colleagues, in the book that borrows for its title Tocqueville's phrase *Habits of the Heart*, found that our "individualism may have grown cancerous" and that even some form of "therapeutic contractualism" may not succeed in the formation of genuine community.[8] Similarly, Sheila Limming states that "the structures of our lives and physical spaces have made atomization rather than community our society's default setting."[9] Such uses of the term "community," however, only underscore the imprecision of the concept and that, as Bellah says, its achievement may be "more an aspiration than a reality." By comparison, Benedict Anderson's seminal study *Imagined Communities*—which, as indicated by its subtitle, *Reflections on the Origin and Spread of Nationalism*, focuses on national groupings—underscores that while the collective portion of the equation is put in terms of "community" such an entity is really viable only at the level of the state.[10] Others, trying to pin down its constituent features, have identified four elements of the "sense of community": *membership*: feeling of belonging or of sharing a sense of personal relatedness; *influence*: mattering, making a difference to a group and of the group mattering to its members; *reinforcement*: integration and fulfillment of needs; and *shared emotional connection*.[11]

Undoubtedly humans acquire substantive orientations from those with whom they share a common situation, and whether one sides with the communitarians who see this as overriding individual impulses or in service to those impulses, in the United States the tension between persons and collectivities comes to the fore mainly when some action is called for.[12] Like other open-ended politicized concepts, community may be played upon by interest groups, whether economic, partisan, or religious.[13] In each instance the concept of community is vague yet always tinged with a sense of longing and of ideals left unfulfilled and—most of all for our purposes—is capable of being brought into the political and legal realms notwithstanding—perhaps because of—those very features. Indeed, the tension between an individual carving out personal attachments and whole sectors of society possessing an identity and powers of their own may be a dilemma that finds it sources in the nature of culture itself. And for that reason it may be valuable to address the dilemma head-on and consider how a revised notion of culture may help us sort out the role of community in both society and law.

Culture's Dilemma and the Indeterminacy of Law

Nowadays the story we are told about human nature is commonly one of biological urges tempered by the idiosyncrasies of personality and environment. Culture, we are assured, is learned if sporadically forgotten, symbols are either intrinsic archetypes or a gratuitous afterthought, and nurture is always trying to catch up with our genetic blueprint.

But there is a better story to be told—more accurate, more comprehensive, and ultimately more poignant. And though few know the tale, it concerns one of the greatest scientific discoveries of the past century.

The year is 1924, the place is South Africa, and the man's name is Raymond Dart. While he was dressing for a friend's wedding, a package arrived from one of Dart's graduate assistants. It contained a skull the student believed to be a hitherto unknown species of early monkey. But Dart's experience as an anatomist led him to suspect it was something far more important. Working laboriously with his wife's knitting needles to release the fossil from the surrounding stone, Dart began to formulate two striking propositions. First, this three-million-year-old australopithecine child did indeed represent a precursor to modern humans; and second (as later evidence was to confirm), these hominins would have been capable of making their own distinctions—whether for fabricating tools or exploiting their habitat—vital to the further evolution of our species.

What Dart grasped, then, was that we essentially cast out instinct and began adapting to our own adaptations. Those hominins whose brains let them see a tool in a block of stone or a plant as edible when cooked increased their chances for survival, which then fueled their ability to create new concepts. Dart thus saw that what is distinctive to being human is the capacity to create the categories of our own experience and that such creativity in turn affected our biological evolution.

Later anthropologists also embraced the idea, formulated as the very definition of culture, that as such categories are fashioned—whether of kinship or food, technology or the sacred—they spread across multiple domains of life—the economic, political, familial, religious—to the point where they seem both immanent and natural. Indeed, it is our ability to use metaphors, in which we grope, crabwise, to link the familiar with the unknown, that makes these naturalized linkages possible. The trick of culture, then, is to make our own creations appear to embrace the world as it is, even as we deal with the world as we imagine it to be. It is a trick, however, that is not without its catch.

The trick itself comes wrapped in a deceptive package. The capacity to classify experience—whether it concerns the colors of the rainbow or the spirits in one's surround—is integral to making a world of the everyday coherent. If you are an insect with only a few days to live you need to know who is mommy and what is edible from the get-go: if you have given up on the categories of experience being innate, you need to fashion them for yourself. Or, more precisely, you *cannot* fashion them for yourself. Thought, which was once enfolded in instinct, now becomes extrinsic, worked upon with others who share your categorizing urge: a "wild child" will not develop language *or* know how to relate to others, being bereft of both instinct *and* culture.[14] Thus in the process of replacing instinct with culture the lingering catch has to be faced.

The snag is revealed when individual capacity and collective need have to be reconciled. The capacity for category distinction is built into every member of our species. At the same time, by forgoing the dictates of instinct and thus not knowing innately who's who and what's what, we need to come to some shared orientation if we are to act collectively—and survive individually. If we were the sort of animal for whom the allocation of tasks was programed into us from the outset the dilemma would not exist. But in our case we need to coordinate our actions with others while retaining our individual capacity to forge new categories and relationships. Absent instinct, the common solution is for people to group together, allocate roles, and treat the resultant assemblages as obvious. But the moment we do that we may limit, unnaturally, the individual propulsion to generate new sets of associations. Thus, with the capacity for culture universally distributed, we may be torn between being organized either from the top down around a leader or creating a structure of roles that would organize us from the ground up. Several solutions are possible. Each, however, only furthers the dilemma.

One solution is indeed to defer to authority to provide order—whether that leadership is grounded in sacred sources, personal magnetism, or the way things have always been done. At the same time, the personal need to keep alive our categorizing capacity as the indispensable tool for adaptation may pull against the existing order. What may seem disorderly in that regard may actually be the very opposite: Terry Pratchett's quip, that "chaos always defeats order because it is better organized," bears more than a grain of truth inasmuch as the human propulsion to generate new combinations constantly revitalizes our ordering capability even as it weakens the status quo. That may also explain why, as Peter Drucker once noted: "Culture eats strategy for breakfast." His point, I think, is that long-term plans commonly give way to underlying assumptions, thereby frustrating the control we imagine has been created once a goal has been formulated. In the process of balancing the individual capacity to reconstruct categories and the collective need to embed them in a regularized life, various approaches have been deployed.

Historically, it has probably been organizing as tribes that has been the most common solution. Tribes, however, are much misunderstood. Far from being exclusionary and pugnacious—and notwithstanding the popular attribution of our fragmented politics to some "tribal" reversion—actual tribes are characterized by several key attributes. Tribes do not like too much power in too few hands for too long a period of time. As a result, tribal powers are divided, conditional, and temporary. A wide range of mechanisms works toward this end. One of the most important—leveling—takes many forms, whether through ritual reversals (where power is relativized by being upended temporarily), structured joking and avoidance patterns (that ease potentially tense relationships), or the deployment of trickster figures (who rejuvenate order even as they undermine it). Similarly, patterns of reciprocity prevent the transformation of material or symbolic capital into overall control. The interchangeability of ways to reciprocate also reinforces the cultural impulse to spread concepts across domains, thereby knitting diverse realms—economic, political, ritual, familial—into a commonsense whole. Fission and fusion, of groups as well as concepts, further reinforce personal category creation just as the frequent adoption of outsiders, multilingualism, and constantly trying on others' cultural attributes are integral to modes of balancing tribal cohesion and individual category construction.[15]

Alternatively, many societies, in the absence of an innate set of roles, have opted—indeed reified—the assignment of various categories of individuals to settled positions. Whether the allocation of roles is done on the basis of race, religion, or ethnicity, the result may be to achieve an organized structure, albeit one that is constantly vulnerable to individual category re-creation. If, for example, race is the chosen vehicle, then those regarded as underlings must not only be readily identifiable by some obvious feature (color, physiognomy, accent); the distinction must also pervade multiple domains of meaning—often rationalized by attributions of inferiority, immorality, or uncleanliness—in order to seem a natural classification. However, unlike insects, who can operate with such innate categories as workers or queens, alpha males or drones, humans cannot be bound to their category assignments unless subjected to force, complicity, or persuasion.

Whatever the ordering arrangement, the tensions pushing toward recombination remain deeply writ in the nature of culture. Several factors are especially important in this regard. Just as metaphor may be a key constituent in relating and naturalizing classifications of our own making, so too ambiguity and ambivalence facilitate our categorizing adaptation. Tribes in particular are incredibly adept at utilizing ambiguity to retain flexibility: more like an amoeba than a crystal, they depend not on settled structures but on the capacity to shape-shift, to form and re-form in response to their environment and their own conceptual history. Like any creature, they may succeed or fail, but their embrace of ambiguity— seen, for example, in their focus on malleable relationships rather than strict rules—gives witness to their recognition that the rage for order and the rage for chaos must offset each other if a culture is to have a chance to survive. Faced with striking such a balance, many Westerners assume that life is characterized by a constant struggle against uncertainty. Indeed, as the journalist Margaret Talbot put it: "Ambivalence is a difficult state of mind to sustain; the temptation to replace it with a more Manichean vision is always close at hand." Nevertheless—and contrary to the stereotype—tribes have a genius for maintaining, even institutionalizing, ambiguity and ambivalence, knowing, perhaps, through eons of experimentation, that doing so limits societal constraints and keeps our individual capacity for culture ready to cope with changing circumstances.

Other tribes, other outcomes. Authoritarian structures, by comparison, may submerge individual category innovation—especially the threat from those preeminent generators of new categories: creative artists, intellectuals, seers—in return for professed stability, while democracies may attempt a balance between the personal and collective with the institutionalized or informal division of powers. By whatever means, however, ambiguity bubbles up to challenge the known while itself being resolved by constantly defining and redefining particular situations. That emphasis on context-as-sorting-mechanism is neatly captured in the words of the narrator in a novel by David Ignatius who says of a central character:

> [He] wasn't a zero or a one. He occupied a space where things were ambiguous, where people are simultaneously friend and foe, loyal and disloyal, impossible to define until the moment when events intervene and force each particle, each heart to one side or the other. A binary separation between black and white might be the human condition, but it wasn't the natural order of things.[16]

Even the seemingly most rigid society must find ways of attending to change, and it is therefore necessary to have a way of approaching circumstances situationally. If all situations are predefined, inherent creativity is frustrated; if each instance is regarded as unique, the predictable behavior of others is problematic. We may tell ourselves that we are adhering to rules and principles, but in fact we are constantly defining the situation and operating on a case-by-case basis to keep our categorizing capacity primed. We do so in the law when we decide matters casuistically or we exercise our categorizing capacity while pretending that uncertainty and judicial discretion are not at work; we do so in our religions when we maintain the open texture of our rituals and grant place of honor to such essentially contested concepts as grace and sin and soul. Each is an attempt to downplay the resurgent force of category creation, and each attempt is only partially successful.

Indeed, since one does not always know how a situation will be characterized and how one's category-creating capacity will become manifest, a paradox exists that is highlighted by Albert O. Hirschman:

> The secret of creativity is then to place yourself in situations where you've got to be creative, but this is done only when one doesn't know in advance that one will have to be creative. This, in turn, is so because we underestimate our creative resources; quite properly, we cannot believe in our creativity until we experience it; and since we thus necessarily underestimate our creative resources we do not consciously engage upon tasks which we know require such resources; hence the only way in which we can bring our creative resources into play is by similarly underestimating the difficulty of a task.[17]

Yet even this contingency does not immobilize our innate propulsion to continue generating meaningful associations. By constantly defining situations with others, we generate and share new categories, thereby bridging to some extent the individual/collective divide. But that only increases the dilemma: imagined collectively, the categories appear not to be the product of a single will but immanent in the nature of things; generated individually, yet having to be enacted with others, they depend for their credibility on our joint endeavors. The kind way to put this is to say that the merger of individual wills creates a sense of impersonal design; the less generous way, incorporated in an old saw, holds that when two fools agree on something it takes on the air of objective truth. The point is that symbol-mongering resides in the individual in place of instinct but, notwithstanding restraints arising from our uncertain assessment of risk, can be effected only when shared, a process that clearly has its own internal strains.

The nature of culture is therefore constantly being tested, but perhaps the present world order underscores the dilemmas and choices that accompany our categorizing nature with particular force. Without institutions of constraint we can lapse into the unconstrained dictator's hands; with too much constraint we violate our cultural nature. The dilemma has hardly passed without notice. Sigmund Freud got it wrong by placing the problem at the level of the psyche (seen as invariably repressed when necessarily confined by culture) rather than where it belongs—as a problem of coordination in a species that requires collective organization to survive but is riven by the individualized generative force of creating new categories that challenge the existing order. In an age of Vladimir Putin and Donald Trump, placing the dangers of our constant quest for distinctions in the hands of those who offer the false resolution of certitude can lead only to even greater strains on our categorizing nature.

The implications for law of this approach to culture are profound. The constant tug between collective coordination and individual meaning may be as integral to the creation of disputes as to their resolution, as central to the formation of rules of engagement as to the consequences of their disruption. For all its appearance of certainty, law remains, in the interstices of procedure and content, somewhat indeterminate, a feature that scholars and jurists have not failed to address. To some that indeterminacy is inherent in the very categories we use to embrace our experiences, an indeterminacy that at once keeps open the adaptability of our conceptualizing capacity and invites engagement with others as we seek that common understanding—or at least passing acquaintance—necessary for orienting and coordinating our actions with others. When, therefore, Edward Levi characterized common law regimes as a "moving system of categorizing concepts," he grasped the essentially open-textured nature of our law.[18] The ramifications of this insight for those who seek certainty in the law are several.

For one, it means that most legal issues are by their nature open-ended but, when they come before the law, may get "unnaturally" foreshortened: a final judgment risks freezing the open texture of the relationships involved and closing off further interaction.[19] But even though such certainty is often momentary and elusive, it does not mean that we cannot recognize a course of action, which for that moment and for that context, feels right for us. Admitting uncertainty thus does not have to be the enemy of decisiveness. Moreover, the recognition that certainty in the law is illusory does not prohibit it from having true consequences. It was in that vein, more than a century ago, that John Dewey argued that our legal system is based on a logic of consequence rather than antecedents, that we do not reason from prior theorems but work back to a general concept from the consequences we envision will flow from our choice.[20] It is in that vein, then, that we have to consider the cultural presuppositions that influence the way we view the facts in a case and the consequences that we imagine will flow from our decisions. And like the case-law approach to grasping general principles, so, too, in our assessment of the place of culture in the law an approach based on concrete cases coupled with a specific form of cultural analysis holds out the prospect of revealing relationships that inform both individual effort and community life.

Case Studies and the Cultural Analysis of Law

Given the ambivalence toward community expressed by Tocqueville and felt so keenly to this day by many Americans, any quest for true community may seem feckless at best. And yet we know that ideals, images, and symbols, even when they do not point to something tangible, nevertheless have real effects. Indeed, perhaps such expressions can be perceived only in their effects, like an atom scrambling through a cloud chamber or a scent that lingers in the mind. Just as ghosts are not real yet belief in them has repercussions that are real, so, too, we ignore the American romance of community at our peril, since the meanings it imparts are real even if the thing itself always seems just out of reach. To grasp community's allure and its far-from-intangible effects, we must have a method for detection. And if it is true, as the saying goes, that "'for example' is no proof," it is equally true that, as Clifford Geertz so wisely said, "there is no ascent to truth without descent to cases." And the method that commends itself under such circumstances is, therefore, one that seeks in the cultural analysis of instances the factors to be considered in any particular case. It is an approach that keeps an eye out for the course taken when individual category creation encounters collective organizational need. One particularly intriguing point of entry is through the law, where distinctions must be made, where imagined relationships and classifications must be enacted, and where at the end of the day decisions must be made.

The consideration of community takes various forms in American law, many of them—like the romance of community itself—being rather indirect. Therefore, the best way to approach such issues is, perhaps, through a series of specific instances rather than through some highly abstract or generalized theory. This is particularly appropriate given the idea of culture that has been indicated, for it allows us to see concrete instances in some detail without professing that they cover all possible cases. The chapters that constitute this book, then, analyze the legal culture of community through just such a set of case studies, with some of the general propositions they embody being highlighted in the process.

I begin in chapter 1 by illuminating how American courts use "the traditions of our people," what "shocks our conscience," and what qualifies as "custom." How integral have these concepts been to the courts' claims of legitimacy and popular support? And if we were to apply a more contemporary concept of culture, how might we fashion a test that adds greater substance and reduces existing subjectivity? If we think of community as held together by cross-domainal categorizations, how might such an interpretation of culture affect our reliance on tradition, conscience, and custom in our law?

Chapter 2 takes on a particular aspect of the law's legitimacy when it asks whether it is possible for judges to express the uncertainty they sometimes feel about a case or principle and whether admitting to such uncertainty is really antithetical to the predictability many regard as indispensable to judicial credibility. Using the statement by John Roberts, the Chief Justice of the United States, about his colleagues' unwillingness to entertain any doubt in the case that overturned fifty years of permitted abortion, we will ask whether the off-the-bench comments by many judges about their own uncertainties must necessarily be kept out of their decisions or may find a useful place within them. We will also have the opportunity to consider the relation between individual and collective creativity in light of the suggestion, as Kenneth Weisbrode puts it, that "so long as we embrace, or at least accept, ambivalence as individuals, we may continue to decry and contain it constructively as a society."[21]

Chapter 3 suggests that the Ninth Amendment's reservation of the unenumerated rights to the people might be interpreted as a vehicle aimed at the preservation of the diversity that is expressed in everything from our national motto to the numerous laws reinforcing our highly differentiated nation. Does such an emphasis entail trusting the individual to make decisions of a very wide range? If so how does one balance that with the role of the state in keeping our personal predilections from undermining our need for collective solidarity? Indeed, how might reliance on the Ninth Amendment bring the law and American culture closer together in such instances as abortion rights?

Chapter 4 asks: Can an entire group be defamed, and not just the individual? Many other legal systems allow actions for group defamation, but the United States does not. Is it the historical context that is crucial to the meaning of such actions? Or is it a question of how the American system has struggled to find a place between the state and the individual for the assertion of group rights more generally? If we value community in some abstract sense, why do we not protect it in some concrete instances? And, once again, would a revised concept of culture aid in addressing this dilemma?

Part II focuses on vulnerable populations. It begins by looking in chapter 5 at the disposition of the remains of native peoples. We will suggest that a special court, not unlike other specialized courts, be set up to adjudicate these issues, a court that could take cultural factors more broadly into consideration than has been the case in courts of general jurisdiction. In the effort to bring native and nonnative communities into a common conversation establishing a forum that is more culturally diverse and procedurally flexible may be part of the solution that has thus far eluded us.

Chapter 6 also concerns native populations, here asking whether the valuation of their cultural artifacts might be more appropriately rendered if the overall role of those objects were part of the equation of their pricing. Is it possible to reconstruct some aspects of intellectual property law to more fully take into account the meaning of such objects within the cultures from which they derive?

Group rights and individual needs come into consideration, too, when, in chapter 7, we look at the way in which the water law of the western United States lost key elements associated with its formal structure of allocation in the process of moving from the cultures of North Africa, where it originated, to its home in the United States. But what would it look like if we were to restore those lost elements? Is such a legal system possible when the cultures are so dissimilar? Or may a legal transplant only succeed if it carries enough of its cultural rootedness with it when it moves? Is the vision of community that informs one culture really transferable? Or is cultural incommensurability our shared fate? In an environment of ever-increasing shortages of the water resource itself, a shortage of consideration for the cultural context of rules may be no less serious an impediment to resolution.

Finally, in chapter 8, if we do focus on the community as possessing certain rights or privileges separate and distinct from either the state or the individual, then how, when investments are made for a charitable institution, is one to fulfill one's duty to individuals and their institutions when risk and reward are being calculated? Such concerns will allow us to draw together some of the broader themes these case studies will have suggested about importing culture into the law in the hope of encouraging further openness to the possibilities of their mutual benefits rather than their separable lives.

* * *

American common law operates with a curious theory. The idea is that if one employs a case-by-case approach coupled with such broad concepts as the rational relation of a legislated law to an acceptable goal, and if one makes changes only very gradually, the acceptance of society, already somewhat ahead of the courts, will reinforce the legitimacy of judicial decisions.[22] It is a curious theory if for no other reason than for its reliance on time being able to bring judgment and practice into accord, its comfortable belief that the status quo is to be preferred over judicial leadership, and its perpetuation of concepts like "the community" as a useful link between judges' actions and the society they profess to follow. In such circumstances, notions like tradition, custom, and conscience serve the dual purpose of fostering a sense of continuity that lies outside individual opinion and bolsters familiar concepts upon which settled attachment, if not settled results, may be imaginatively based. Like a precipitate that surfaces and recedes as circumstances vary, community as a concept is as vital when dormant as it is when emergent; like any other myth it is as real as it is imagined. And because community lives in its particularities, it is there that we must go in search of it.

PART I

Bringing Community into the Law

1

Identifying the Indefinable

"Tradition," "Conscience," "Custom"

Today, the Court purports to be the dispassionate oracle of
the law, unmoved by "natural sympathy."
Justice Harry Blackmun, dissenting, *DeShaney v. Winnebago
County DSS*, 489 U.S. 189 (1989)

Judges commonly act like oracles. They portray the law as speaking through
them, rather than them speaking through the law. The process may incorporate justifications based on religion, logic, status, or nature, but, in
whatever form, the image of neutrality aims to cover, at best, the sense of
uncertainty that goes with judging others or, at worst, the belief in oneself
or one's legal system as inerrant. Self-delusion may displace self-awareness:
Harvard Law School professor Lon Fuller, for example, could propound
the patently absurd syllogism that good is logical while evil is not, that the
common law is logical, therefore the common law always yields good. In an
attempt to remove oneself from one's judging, recourse may also be had to
other factors said to lie outside the self. Among these, at least in the American system of legal rhetoric and decision-making, are tradition, conscience,
and custom. Each may or may not correlate with a particular political orientation, but each resides as a vital, if inexact, basis for judgments that seek
not to appear as being of the judges' own making.

In this chapter we will consider what courts have meant when they refer
to—indeed ground their rulings on—"the traditions of our people," actions
that "shock the conscience," and judgments that rely on the "customs" of a
group. Are these concepts merely in the eye of the beholding judge or do
they—could they—be more solidly grounded if we were to apply a more
culturally based conception of each of them? Indeed, could these recon-
figured concepts ally more closely than before with those aspects of "community" to which the law also professes attachment?

* * *

> Tradition! Without our traditions our lives would be as shaky as . . . as a
> Fiddler on the Roof!
> Tevya, *Fiddler on the Roof*

We know what the term "tradition" imports—a lengthy course of conduct that is frequently used either to direct others along a well-trodden path or to justify new actions as if they were the natural continuance of what went before.[1] But we also know that traditions may be the subject of instant creation, whether it is the Scottish kilt that was actually invented in the eighteenth century or the claim to nationhood based on a manufactured pedigree.[2] (I once had a strenuous discussion with one of my Princeton University students who, following a classroom discussion about campus rituals, insisted that the practice of running naked in the quad at the first snowfall was an ancient university tradition. When I suggested that I had been at the university long enough to have seen that it developed only with co-education and that boys running naked in front of other boys would hardly have held the same meaning as it did after the arrival of women students, she was adamant in wanting the event to be justified by age-old practice.) And certainly Max Weber had a point when he noted that tradition—as a claim that things have always been done this way—is one of the classic means by which the powerful lay claim to legitimate control. While critical matters of politics and religion undoubtedly turn on such assertions, it is, perhaps, when tradition is called upon by the law that its power may be most immediately felt.

American judges of quite different persuasions have frequently asked whether the issue before them is "deeply rooted in the nation's history and tradition." References of this sort gained force with the 1952 U.S. Supreme Court decision in *Rochin v. California* when Justice Felix Frankfurter, speaking for the majority, wrote:

> Regard for the requirements of the Due Process Clause "inescapably imposes upon this Court an exercise of judgment upon the whole course of the proceedings [resulting in a conviction] in order to ascertain whether they offend those canons of decency and fairness which express the notions of justice of English-speaking peoples even toward those charged

with the most heinous offenses." These standards of justice are not authoritatively formulated anywhere as though they were specifics. Due process of law is a summarized constitutional guarantee of respect for those personal immunities which, as Mr. Justice Cardozo twice wrote for the Court, are "so rooted in the traditions and conscience of our people as to be ranked as fundamental," or are "implicit in the concept of ordered liberty."[3]

Over the decades Supreme Court decisions that have referred to tradition, like those referring to history, have continued to mount. A number of justices on various sides of the political spectrum accepted and employed the concept. Justice Lewis Powell, for example, wrote in a case challenging the exclusion of extended families from living in an area zoned for single-family dwelling units: "Our decisions establish that the Constitution protects the sanctity of the family precisely because the institution of the family is deeply rooted in this Nation's history and tradition."[4] So, too, Justice Antonin Scalia, in *Michael H. v. Gerald D.*, argued that our traditions preclude treating a natural father the same as the husband of the wife for purposes of gaining parental rights.[5] However, the dissent by Justices William Brennan, Thurgood Marshall, and Harry Blackmun argued that using "tradition" to read due process narrowly is incorrect: "Apparently oblivious to the fact that this concept can be as malleable and as elusive as 'liberty' itself, the plurality pretends that tradition places a discernible border around the Constitution."[6]

As for the concern that the uses of tradition will simply reflect the political perspectives of the various judges, it should also be recalled that in 1996 Justice Scalia, writing the only dissenting opinion in a case that ended the 157-year tradition of state-supported, all-male education at Virginia Military Institute, said: "[T]he tradition of having government funded military schools for men is as well rooted in the traditions of this country as the tradition of sending only men into military combat. The people may decide to change the one tradition, like the other, through democratic processes; but the assertion that either tradition has been unconstitutional through the centuries is not law, but politics smuggled into law."[7]

More recently, in *Dobbs v. Jackson Women's Health Organization*, which overturned the abortion decision in *Roe v. Wade*, justices on both sides invoked the word "tradition" forty-seven times, while in a Second Amendment gun case "tradition" as national history appeared fifty-one times.[8] By invoking such references several things may be happening: the case-by-case method is actually creating an index of actual instances that can be fit under the rubric of tradition, one unknown is simply being replaced with another, or some form of cherry-picking is being employed to reach a predetermined end. As for the first possibility, it is typical of the common law to establish a broad rubric, fill it with concrete instances, and then abandon the typology as new cases challenge the existing categories' capacity to persuade. As for replacing one unknown with another it is hard to ignore what John Dewey once said of educational tests, namely, that they reminded him of the way they weigh hogs down in Texas. You get a long plank, he said, and after throwing it over a crossbar you tie the hog to one end of the plank and a rock that balances the hog onto the other end. Then you all stand around and try to guess how much the rock weighs!

Cherry-picking examples also has its dangers. When it comes to choosing historical instances, the Supreme Court's gun-control decision in *New York State Rifle & Pistol Association Inc. v. Bruen* is particularly noteworthy. That case abandons the long prevalent approach of balancing the public interest against personal liberties in favor of a "historical tradition" test. Writing for the majority, Justice Clarence Thomas, who uses the word "tradition" twenty-five times in his opinion, stated: "The government must affirmatively prove that its firearms regulation is part of the historical tradition that delimits the outer bounds of the right to keep and bear arms."[9] Quite aside from the ruling occasioning a good deal of employment for historians who are now combing ancient records to justify or limit additional gun rights, the emphasis on such traditions underscores how readily one may pick and choose among past practices in the name of maintaining a community's identity and integrity. "But," as Justice Stephen Breyer, following his own lengthy analysis of the history of American gun legislation, noted in dissent, "the Court does not say how many cases or laws would suffice 'to show a tradition of public-carry regulation.'"[10]

In brief, the use of tradition as a basis of judicial decision-making cannot avoid the twinned dilemmas of duration and scope. How long is long enough for something to qualify as a tradition? How much must it govern relevant situations to be considered a settled course of governance? By how many people? And how much does recourse to "tradition" actually reflect contemporary values and politics? However, instead of lining up a series of incidents in an attempt to thread together chronology and circumstance—or to use such selections to justify current political views—might there be a better way to conceptualize the practices of a culture such that while legal answers do not emerge as self-evident a somewhat more appropriate test for concepts like tradition might be workable? Before suggesting such an approach, it may be useful to add the two other concepts so often found in American legal opinions—conscience and custom—in order to flesh out the overall problem.

***

A man's conscience and his judgment is the same thing; and as the judgment, so also the conscience, may be erroneous.
Thomas Hobbes, *Leviathan*, 311

In *Rochin* Justice Frankfurter connected tradition to conscience when he wrote: "[W]e are compelled to conclude that the proceedings by which this conviction was obtained do more than offend some fastidious squeamishness or private sentimentalism about combatting crime too energetically. This is conduct that shocks the conscience."[11] Arguing that the concept of conscience, when enfolded within the Due Process Clause of the Constitution, is not imprecise, he wrote:

The vague contours of the Due Process Clause do not leave judges at large. We may not draw on our merely personal and private notions and disregard the limits that bind judges in their judicial function. Even though the concept of due process of law is not final and fixed, these limits are derived from considerations that are fused in the whole nature of our judicial process. These are considerations deeply rooted in reason and in the compelling traditions of the legal profession. The Due Process Clause places upon this Court the duty of exercising a judgment, within the narrow confines of judicial power in reviewing State convictions, upon interests of society pushing in opposite directions.[12]

Rochin is hardly unique: A search of Lexis-Nexis shows that courts have used the phrase "shocks the conscience" in one context or another on hundreds of occasions.[13] In many instances the courts appear to be seeking the outer limits of acceptable behavior. So, for example, they have found it shocking when a police officer, suspecting an individual of having swallowed drugs in order to hide them, forces the individual to regurgitate the contents of his stomach. Or a court may find that an excessive award by a jury shocks the conscience if the jurors were swayed by emotionally provocative evidence. The applicability of the concept as it concerns state actors is summarized in *Isaacs v. Konawa Public Schools*: "Executive action that shocks the conscience requires much more than negligence. Conduct that shocks the judicial conscience . . . is deliberate government action that is 'arbitrary' and 'unrestrained by the established principles of private right and distributive justice.' To show a defendant's conduct is conscience shocking, a plaintiff must prove a government actor arbitrarily abused his authority or employed it as an instrument of oppression."[14] But are not all these terms inherently vague and thus subject to the whims of whichever judge applies them?

To the argument that "conscience," like "tradition," is indeed wholly subjective, Justice Felix Frankfurter responded:

> Restraints on our jurisdiction are self-imposed only in the sense that there is from our decisions no immediate appeal short of impeachment or constitutional amendment. But that does not make due process of law a matter of judicial caprice. The faculties of the Due Process Clause may be indefinite and vague, but the mode of their ascertainment is not self-willed. In each case "due process of law" requires an evaluation based on a disinterested inquiry pursued in the spirit of science, on a balanced order of facts exactly and fairly stated, on the detached consideration of conflicting claims, on a judgment not *ad hoc* and episodic but duly mindful of reconciling the needs both of continuity and of change in a progressive society.[15]

Although concurring in the decision, two of Frankfurter's colleagues objected to his eliding legal tradition, conscience, and Western practices. Justice Hugo Black found that reliance on notions of decency, fairness, and the English-speaking world's idea of justice is not only vague and ethnocentric but also risks overturning explicit constitutional rights in the name of some inchoate and subjective judgment.[16] Similarly, Justice William O. Douglas found that Frankfurter's criteria leave matters to "the idiosyncrasies of the judges" and constitute "part of the process of erosion of civil rights of the citizen."[17]

In the decades since *Rochin* lower courts have, therefore, found themselves in something of a bind. They have tried to give the "shocks the conscience" test some regularity, stating, for example, that when the legislature treads on a fundamental right they need to justify their action in the light of very strict scrutiny by the court, but that when the executive does so they must *also* show that what has been done "shocks the conscience," presumably granting the latter somewhat greater leeway in the process. Thus, either the action involved must be so egregious as to overstep the limits almost anyone would acknowledge or the matter remains intensely subjective, as Justices Black and Douglas implied. And if the assessment is rather subjective, is that not precisely why we vet judges for their temperament and restraint when we appoint them and are thereafter compelled to rely on their judgment and wisdom?

So, the dilemma persists. Is shocking the conscience like knowing pornography when you see it?[18] If a police officer's conduct is shocking for forcing a suspect to regurgitate an illicit drug, what if the suspect had swallowed a slip of paper indicating the location of an entombed kidnap victim with only hours of oxygen remaining? Are there only limiting cases? Or does recourse to the language of conscience have some broadly shared foundational content? If it is not possible to eradicate all judicial subjectivity, is it possible to specify some of the parameters by which the concept of conscience might be given more regularity? Adding the third concept—custom—may help in addressing these issues.

* * *

Customs tell a man who he is, where he belongs, what he must do.
Better illogical customs than none; men cannot live together without them.
Robert A. Heinlein, *Citizen of the Galaxy*

[H]e is a barbarian, and thinks that the customs of his tribe and island are the laws of nature.
George Bernard Shaw, *Caesar and Cleopatra*

> Laws change more slowly than custom, and though dangerous when they fall behind the times are more dangerous still when they presume to anticipate custom.
>
> Marguerite Yourcenar, *Memoires of Hadrian*

American law is not tone-deaf to custom. Indeed, like many legal systems (albeit in quite different ways), the courts reach out directly to it in various contexts; "custom and usage in the trade," for example, is a well-established concept, wherein a court may incorporate in its opinion the approach of practitioners of a given craft or trade. So, for example, when international wire transfers of money were first introduced and the question as to whether the rate of exchange was that of the point of departure or the point of arrival, courts turned to the people in the trade and basically adopted their custom. Similarly, the question of a railroad's liability for injury to a worker was settled by looking at what the workers regularly do and not simply what one or another party claimed as their responsibility following an accident. But whereas in the European tradition custom is conceived as quite separate from law until it is brought within the ambit of the law and then becomes law, in the United States the two are largely kept conceptually separate even when the courts essentially incorporate custom. As in the other concepts we have mentioned, history matters.

Not surprisingly, the concept and role of custom in American law have changed over the course of time, as have the rationales on which custom is based and discoverable. The issues that confront an appropriate role for custom in the law have deep and enduring roots. Like many since, the Glossators, who revived Roman law in the eleventh to twelfth centuries, were perplexed by custom when they asked whether it is subsidiary to or rules over statutory law. Emperor Julian had argued that the difference is not significant, "for what does it matter whether the people declares its will by vote or by circumstances and conduct?"[19] The Glossators settled on ten to twenty years for something to constitute custom but added that there had to be one or two "acts of usage," which really came down to several courts recognizing the custom. But uncertainties remained. If popular support is vital to applying custom, is it enough if important people, who the public will follow, are involved in the cases that seek its recognition? Can the lawyers who argue for the custom be regarded as stand-ins for the people? And how would one show that a majority of people do indeed acknowledge, much less abide by, the purported custom?

Later commenters took quite varied positions on the matter. The French legal scholar François Gény (1861–1959), whose advocacy of judicial discretion in the interpretation of statutory law had an important influence across Europe, was skeptical as to how and by whom the users of a custom could be determined, while critics like his countryman, legal realist Marcel Planiol (1853–1931), argued that custom is just what the courts say it is, thus yielding "a customary law of recent creation."[20] Like others before and since, many commenters were also concerned whether certain segments of the population might claim custom as a way of getting around general laws, and many have remained dubious as to how one can ever show that judicial opinions actually reflect the popular, rather than the influential, will.

More recent scholarship has turned for answers to economic and psychological theories. Whereas many of the late-nineteenth-century commenters suggested that the law was always a step behind custom and as such might stultify the "living" nature of custom, contemporary scholarship has tended to concentrate on measuring costs and benefits against some primal economic theory or relying on psychological theories of personal advantage.[21] Whether one takes a customary practice as dispositive or only as evidence to be laid alongside other considerations, recourse to proffered economic forces and psychological dispositions may lead to claims of "neutral" analysis that place boundaries around the relevant and predispose the choice of facts.[22] In doing so, custom once again becomes vulnerable to claims of the "scientific" study of law irrespective of the scope of inquiry and the politics of resultant choices.

Reliance on custom is, in fact, often a function of one's broader political philosophy. If the law is seen as a living thing that must keep up with change, custom may be the vehicle of preference for spotting those alterations; if custom is taken as a necessary restraint on change, then the rationale may be that expressed by Russell Kirk, the political commenter whose 1953 book *The Conservative Mind* helped shape the present era of American conservative thought, who listed custom as one of his canons of conservative thought: "Custom, convention, and old prescription are checks both upon man's anarchic impulse and upon the innovator's lust for power."[23] Whatever their position on the political spectrum, an underlying orientation toward one or another theory of how society works or should work risks being self-satisfyingly supportive of one's predisposition rather than being based on the most thoughtful analysis of alternative interpretations of the role of custom in the larger context of a cultural system.

Many of the issues that arise for the adoption of custom as grounds for a legal decision are thus shared with the related concepts of tradition and conscience: each in its own way asks how widespread the practice must be and how long it has been around. There are some differences among the three concepts: whereas courts do not normally reach out to specialists to inform it as to what is shocking to the conscience and, for all their use of history, do not simply defer to professional historians to determine for them the relevance of tradition, a showing of custom depends much more on the expert opinions brought to the court. Nevertheless, duration, spread, and intensity of acceptance of a custom remains largely indeterminate and thus the bounds of relevance for its recognition remain closely controlled by the bench. Given that such concepts will always remain "essentially contested," subject to personal interpretations and agendas, and be grounded in some theory of their nature and import—and given that there are inherent problems with each of the approaches noted and no single approach that can claim irrefutable truth—it may help to at least consider a more appropriate theory of culture upon which to carry forward the bearing of tradition, conscience, and custom on the well-being of any community.

* * *

Tradition, conscience, custom—each incorporates an appraisal of the practices and values of a diverse population for which neither the use of surveys nor professional opinion is always practicable or supportive of judicial credibility. Each also makes certain assumptions about the community, that is, whether it does indeed have discernible commonalities or its multifarious embodiments require restatement by an oracular tribunal. But just as American law was significantly affected—indeed, improved—by the use of the well-known Brandeis brief, which expanded the scope of relevant economic and social information and thereby led to significantly new ways of thinking about both fact and law, so, too, a more refined consideration of culture may improve the application of all three of these concepts.[24] Without displacing precedent and constitutional tests one might therefore add a cultural test that could better inform courts that continue to seek what passes in a community for tradition, conscience, and custom.

To see how a revised concept of culture might be helpful, we need to start with the insight noted in the introduction to this book that human beings are essentially category-creating creatures. Having all but driven out instinct and replaced it with the capacity to create the categories of our own experience, humans take one step further and proliferate these categories across multiple domains—the economic, familial, religious, legal—in order to make these concepts feel coherent and meaningful. So, for example, the idiom of kinship may be naturalized by rendering the Almighty a father, the citizenry a family, the faithful an assembly of brothers and sisters. Indeed, for a concept to do its work, it must link the otherwise separable domains of our lives so as to appear both imminent and natural. While that integration is never perfect or perceived in the same way and to the same level of intensity by all members of the culture, it must be sufficiently shared to make orienting one's actions toward others with an adequate degree of their predictable response for social life to be possible. If, then, we test not simply for the presence of a concept but also for the telltale signs of its pervasiveness across domains—if, in short, we look for its resonance in multiple aspects of our lives—we may be able to make a better case for its constituting a tradition, its disruption constituting a violation of our collective conscience, or its presence so knitting together the disparate elements of our experience as to constitute a cognizable custom. Sometimes referred to as the "thick description" of a culture, as a pattern or structure, such cultural assemblages may not be subject to a precise litmus test but they are so integral to the sense of orderliness of a culture as to be both recognizable and capable of legitimate implementation.[25] Indeed, there are two components of this cultural test that a court could consider, which may be denominated the "multiplex" and the "semiotic" prongs.

The multiplex test consists of demonstrating to a reasonable level that whatever practice is at issue does indeed cross multiple domains of the culture. In his classic formulation of the concept, Max Gluckman argued that in many societies people have multiple and cross-cutting relationships with one another, such that a workmate may simultaneously be a neighbor, belong to the same church, have children who attend the same school, and share in certain rituals. That fact alone, he notes, may be "an important source of quarrels and conflict; but it is equally the basis of internal cohesion in any society."[26] While American relationships are frequently one-off, transactional, and even impersonal, the acceptance of at least passing acquaintance with one another's orientations is indispensable to civil engagement. If a court is serious about looking for a practice to qualify as either traditional, customary, or such as to shock the conscience, it would be well-advised, at the very least, to take evidence that the practice is one that crosses the multiple ways in which people may be tied to one another. Absent such evidence, recourse should not be had to such rationales for the resolution of a legal case. When there is prima facie evidence that a practice does indeed appear to inform relationships in multiple domains, the second prong of the test comes into play.

The second prong—the semiotic test—notes that categories are embraced in language and symbols and that if a concept is indeed broadly shared it will show itself in the terms we use to make it known to ourselves and one another. As the "material vehicles of thought" (to borrow Clifford Geertz's famous characterization), symbols carry a culture's understanding of the categories through which shared experience is organized. To group kinsmen or sacred moments, to classify eatables and the forbidden, to stratify by caste or class or color is to give solidity to the arbitrary and reality to the imagined. Moreover, because the categories through which members of a culture communicate their shared orientations are embodied in such symbols, it is possible to unpack them and see both their logic and their functions. For a court of law to test for scope and commonality not by its own lights or even by survey or statistics but by receiving information about the cultural scheme through which a grasp of collective experience is incorporated into language and symbols would offer a more refined sense of what is shared, toward what ends, and to what extent than does taking unrelated examples from diverse moments in a nation's history or relying upon the judge's sensibilities to give structure to a decision that is, in fact, largely subjective.

Consider how this test might be applied in several cases. The idea of the state intruding into one's body is surely a concept that finds little resonance in a multiplicity of domains—religious, parental, economic—

and is hedged by personal permission (in the medical or relational contexts) or by parental oversight of a minor. Neither is such intrusion sanctioned by the second prong of the test: a set of positively regarded symbolic or linguistic encapsulations. Whether we view it as tradition or conscience, such invasiveness finds little if any support in the cultural criteria suggested. In the realm of tort, if workers are thought to protect one another, one may ask: Does that custom not express itself in religion, in our image of the heroic, in our expectations of assistance from a neighbor, as well as in the actuality of coming to another's aid in times of risk? A court that seeks the cross-cutting attachments and symbolic expressions of such expectations will be able to point to some concrete cultural basis rather than to its own perception of what may be called a "tradition" or "custom." Other examples can be found in family law. Family law has been changing drastically over the past generation, with same-sex marriage being constitutionally recognized, surrogate parenthood acknowledged, assisted suicide possible in some places, and the right of a teenager to change sexual identity reconceptualized. But just as the word "gay" became pervasive when popular culture recognized its public existence and many religions altered their viewpoints, a court could well have noted that all elements of the above test were met, thus supporting its legal recognition in a variety of contexts. In each of these instances it is not only how widespread or time-honored a proposition is that matters but also how pervasive a practice is across cultural domains and symbolic forms. Findings along these lines would, therefore, sidestep judicial discretion as the source for recognition of a community's standards.

In a sense the claim put forth here might appear as an attempt to replace judges with anthropologists. And while such expertise may have some merit, the lesson is not one of deferring to expertise but relying on little more than what one learned in Anthropology 101. We use tests of science (fingerprints, DNA) in our pursuit of facts, we use economic theories in our legal decisions to compare risk, and we rely on expert psychologists in determinations of capacity to stand trial or to assess the applicability of an insanity defense. So, it is hardly out of the question to apply a simple anthropological test for cultural integrity. The criteria suggested here are no more vague than other legal tests—strict scrutiny, reasonable doubt, preponderance of the evidence, and so on—and the case-by-case approach of the common law will help to fill up the new criteria with substantive experience. In doing so we will not eradicate judicial discretion much less established rights. Instead, by bringing culture into the law through an updated concept of how culture is deployed, we may be able to add further precision to the concepts of tradition, conscience, and custom and thereby render our decisions closer to the actual experiences of a nation's changing sense of community.

2

"Left at Large"

The Supreme Court and the Death of Uncertainty

How can a judge who is not entirely sure of the wisdom or consequences of his or her judgment give voice to that uncertainty in a system that calls for definitive answers? Of course, one could say that the legal case is limited to the narrow issue or facts presented, that the jury or lower court is really responsible for deciding the matter, or that the issues may be revisited at a later time as new variations arise. But some recognition of uncertainty is not necessarily unhealthy: Ambivalence is not the same as unresponsiveness, ambiguity is not the equivalent of indecision, and doubt may be appropriate to the indeterminate.

In this chapter we will see how uncertainty plays out in the jurisprudence of some judges on and off the bench, even when their remarks underscore the dilemma without offering a means for its resolution. In particular we will ask: What would it do to the legitimacy of a court if such expressions of doubt were to be incorporated in decisions? And is it not possible for the law to avail itself of the benefits of doubt without sliding into the depths of uncertainty?

* * *

> To practice the requisite detachment and to achieve sufficient objectivity no doubt demands of judges the habit of self-discipline and self-criticism, incertitude that one's own views are incontestable and alert tolerance toward views not shared. But these are precisely the presuppositions of our judicial process. They are precisely the qualities society has a right to expect from those entrusted with ultimate judicial power.
> Justice Felix Frankfurter, *Rochin v. California*[1]

In a stunning—and largely unnoticed—passage in his concurring opinion in *Dobbs v. Jackson Women's Health Organization*, the Supreme Court decision that overturned *Roe v. Wade*, Chief Justice John Roberts wrote: "Both the Court's opinion and the dissent display a relentless freedom from doubt on the legal issue that I cannot share." In those few words the Chief Justice sounded the death knell for uncertainty in the law.

Though few have been so candid in acknowledging it, doubt is an issue with which judges have long struggled. One judge who owned up to the problem was Learned Hand, often referred to as the most influential judge who never served on the Supreme Court. The case that came before three members of the federal court of appeals in 1947 involved an application for citizenship from a man who, years earlier in his native Belgium, had smothered his hopelessly malformed infant son. The law then (as now) said that citizenship can be denied if an applicant is not "of good moral character."[2] At that time homosexuals, for example, were regarded as lacking such character. But what of someone who engaged in euthanasia?

In a letter sent to Hand by his close friend Felix Frankfurter, the Supreme Court justice wrote: "I await with eagerness bordering on impatience your opinion," the question being: "[T]o what extent may a judge assume that his own notions of right moral standards are those of the community?" Jerome Frank, the well-known legal realist and fellow judge in the case, thought the answer should lie with "the attitude of our ethical leaders." Learned Hand, however, found that unconvincing. Clearly uncertain, Hand followed his account of the facts in the case with an anguished statement: "[L]eft at large as we are, without means of verifying our conclusion, and without authority to substitute our individual beliefs, the outcome must needs be tentative; and not much is gained by discussion." He later wrote to Frankfurter: "Oh Jesus! I don't know how we are supposed to deal with such cases except by the best guess we have."[3]

While such candid admissions of uncertainty are relatively rare, hesitant expressions of doubt by judges are not unprecedented, as in recent cases involving the timeline of mail-in ballots, the history of the Second Amendment, or the constitutionality of a no-fly list. Indeed, doubt has been commended by a wide range of thinkers. "Doubt," said Voltaire, "is an uncomfortable position. But certainty is an absurd one";[4] "fifty doubts are better than one certainty," say the Muslim rationalists. Judges, too, have lauded the benefits of doubt: "To have doubted one's own first principles is the mark of a civilized man," admonished Justice Oliver Wendell Holmes, Jr.; "[W]e must remember that [certainty] is not the only good, that we can buy it at too high a price," wrote Justice Benjamin Cardozo.[5] But while others may rest on their doubts, for members of the Supreme Court in particular, as the Welsh saying goes, "at the end you must judge." Indeed, American law forces the illusion of certainty by its binary demands—guilty/innocent, liable/not liable, rights acknowledged/rights denied. To fully assess the place of doubt and uncertainty, much depends on what it is you seek to accomplish through the law and by what means. This is where both philosophy and comparative legal studies enter the picture.

The British philosopher H. L. A. Hart once put the problem succinctly: for any legal system, he said, "the first handicap is our relative ignorance of fact; the second is our relative indeterminacy of aim."[6] For Hart, our very language is responsible for such uncertainty: "rules [possess] a fringe of vagueness or 'open texture,' [and since] nothing can eliminate this duality of a core of certainty and a penumbra of doubt" the best we can do is factor out those cases that seem most certain and find some middle ground for all the rest.[7] So as concerns the facts, one can in criminal law, for example, set various levels of proof ("beyond a reasonable doubt," "by a preponderance of the evidence") or see facts in the light most favorable to a defendant, thereby raising the bar for the state to prove guilt; in constitutional cases one may call for a rational relation between a statute and its goal or raise the barrier piecemeal to the level of such strict scrutiny that a fundamental right may survive almost any abrogation. German law, for example, sets the standard of proof in many cases at "certainty," but neither in Continental nor in common law regimes does certainty or doubt ever receive clear definition or unswerving application. Alternatively, one may rely on witnesses, experts, or the ordinary juror to deal with uncertain facts—wary, however, that each may have some personal or professional bias.

Similar issues arise for Hart's "indeterminacy of aim." One may try to cope with the uncertainty of purpose by considering many goals to which the legal process may aspire. Compromise has its merits, but sometimes at the cost of a genuine right; reconciliation may be socially commended, but resentment may linger in the absence of a mutually beneficial relationship. In addition, principles may not develop if conciliation displaces published opinions and respect for precedent. Alternatively, one may see law's goal not as the articulation of inalienable rights but as support for the duties owed each citizen to society. However, the emphasis on rights raises perplexing questions about their actual source (natural law, public opinion, the "traditions or conscience of our people"), while the insistence on duties may stumble into absolutism.

Clearly there is need for a reasonably high degree of certainty in many domains of the law. In business one may need to have a significant degree of predictability as to the rules of contracts that will garner enforcement; in criminal law one must know what actions may threaten punishment; and in family law marriage regulations or custodial apportionment must not be deeply ambiguous.[8] But a very high level of certainty is not equally applicable to all questions that may arise before a court. True, a court may restrict its opinion very narrowly in order to avoid speaking to a range of factual situations all at once, or judges may simply avoid taking a case when a decision may only muddy the waters. Nevertheless, owning up to uncertainty while still deciding a matter is not the same as creating chaos. To the contrary, it may have healthy benefits. Acknowledging uncertainty might prompt potential litigants to look toward one another to resolve the matter; it may realistically acknowledge that context may matter more than principle; it may commend greater attention to revising existing laws rather than applying outdated rules in the name of some imagined stability. The question, as always, is one of balance, a balance the American legal system may exacerbate rather than resolve by pretending to more than it can deliver.

In a sense, then, it would seem that Americans have boxed themselves in, marshaling all of the apparatus necessary to maintain the appearance of certainty, whether by claiming that it resides only in what is explicit in the Constitution—itself raised to the level of Sacred Text—or imagining that following precedent eradicates politics. Myths, as anthropologists have long argued, serve as a charter for the allocation of power and render the worlds we create as immanent and natural. We Americans grant ourselves a false security, as Douglas Adams notes in *The Hitchhiker's Guide to the Galaxy*: "We demand rigidly defined areas of doubt and uncertainty!" Not surprisingly, our judges may appear either schizophrenic (when their formal decisions do not square with their off-the-bench remarks) or simply hypocritical.[9] But even if one probes beyond the stories we tell ourselves and the fear that uncertainty undermines legitimacy, it might seem that we have no alternative but to choose up sides. Some of the ways courts have coped with doubt may, however, offer, if not a path between what is certain and what is open to question, then at least a waypoint on the road to a shared sense of the workable, itself an indispensable element to the fashioning of a common sense of community. Nowhere is this more suggestive than in the abortion decisions.

In certain respects *Roe v. Wade* was an exercise in coping with uncertainty. The decision is, however, often misconstrued. To understand the case fully we must return to the summer of 1972 when Justice Harry Blackmun, who was to author the majority opinion in the case, went back to his native Minnesota to continue with the research his clerks had already begun that spring.

Blackmun had grown up in St. Paul, and after his undergraduate and law studies at Harvard and some years of private practice he became legal counsel to the Mayo Clinic. Described at times as "risk averse"[10] and by his hometown newspaper as "a tense man" with "his own inner demons,"[11] he once said that in the law "not all is black and white,"[12] that he was "not untroubled" in an important labor case,[13] that death penalty cases "provide for me an excruciating agony of the spirit,"[14] and (before his complete rejection of it in *Callins v. Collins*[15]) that "I have also expressed doubts about whether . . . capital punishment remains constitutional at all."[16]

Religion, too, would seem to have played a role in his approach to doubt. Blackmun was a deeply committed Methodist who was seen on occasion to be weeping during worship.[17] The method in Methodism includes working through doubt to belief—indeed, not seeing the one as anathema to the other. His church's approach to abortion would seem to resonate with that theme and Blackmun's own lack of certainty on the issue. The United Methodist Church's official position on abortion, as set forth in the *Book of Discipline*, states: "Our belief in the sanctity of unborn human life makes us reluctant to approve abortion. But we are equally bound to respect the sacredness of the life and well-being of the mother and the unborn child."[18] Blackmun, perhaps as a result of his years working with doctors at the Mayo Clinic, initially appeared to be somewhat more concerned with the protection from criminal liability of her doctor than with the rights of the pregnant woman.[19] But as he became involved with women's rights more generally he moved from saying of *Roe* that "[t]he decision vindicates the right of the physician to administer treatment according to his professional judgment"[20] to emphasizing that

> few decisions are more personal and intimate, more properly private, or more basic to individual dignity and autonomy, than a woman's decision—with the guidance of her physician and within the limits specified in Roe—whether to end her pregnancy. A woman's right to make that choice freely is fundamental. Any other result, in our view, would protect inadequately a central part of the sphere of liberty that our law guarantees equally to all.[21]

Blackmun was aided in that transition—indeed, in his overall encounter with uncertainty—by the results of the research he had done before drafting the opinion in *Roe*.

Blackmun's research came against a background of having been warned by several of his colleagues on the Court not to express his misgivings in the cases before them. Chief Justice Warren Burger, Blackmun's boyhood friend and intermittent ally, had asked him to "consider some "muting'"[22] in those hard cases where Blackmun had expressed himself "inadequate and hesitant,"[23] while Justice Hugo Black had counseled him: "Always go for the jugular. Never agonize in an opinion. Make it sound as though it's just as clear as crystal."[24] But in *Roe*—as in the death penalty cases—Blackmun was uncomfortable following his colleagues' advice. Instead, his research led him to deal with uncertainty by noting that major religions had changed their approach to abortion over time and that, given such uncertainty, decisions should be left, at least in the first trimester, to the woman and her doctor, the state's interest increasing only as greater possibility for the fetus's survival increases. He came to this conclusion in no small part as a result of his time back at the Mayo Clinic, an effort that led him to "an awareness of medical history I have not had before." But his research also led to an increased awareness of how different religions had changed their positions over time.

A large part of Blackmun's opinion covers the religious history of abortion, a section most law casebooks condense or eliminate entirely.

But for the Justice this history was important to the legal question: Who must bear the burden of proof and to what level? The analysis cast in these terms goes something like this. The rights of an adult are known, but those of a fetus are in dispute. In such uncertain cases the law characteristically asks: Who has to prove which entity's rights are superior, and how high a level of certainty must their claim achieve? Since an adult's rights to bodily integrity are known and those of the fetus are not, the burden properly falls to those questioning the existing person's rights as inferior to those whose rights have yet to be determined. And since whoever must prove unknown rights are superior to known rights will fail in that endeavor, the woman's rights must prevail. The point of Blackmun's extensive review of the history of abortion was, therefore, to show that neither religion nor science has proven that purported fetal rights are superior to the known rights of an adult and accordingly those of the latter must take precedence. While this might seem to suggest that the woman's right to an abortion should be absolute—in notes under the heading "The state purpose rationale" he stated: "Historically there was no barrier. The state has no traditional interest"[25]—the Justice and six of his colleagues, though preferring different positions on when the state may intervene, found that the woman's rights prevailed at least during an initial period of the pregnancy, the precise nature and scope of the state's interest beyond that point being left unaddressed. In a cover letter accompanying his draft opinion, Blackmun wrote to his colleagues: "You will observe that I have concluded that the end of the first trimester is crucial. This is arbitrary, but perhaps any other selected point, such as quickening or viability, is equally arbitrary."[26] The question remains whether it was the implications for state power or the implications of constitutionalizing women's rights generally that led the majority to the compromise trimester rule.

If the majority in *Roe* confronted uncertainty by splitting the difference, other judges have needed a form of indivisible certainty. For originalists (including later members of the Court like Antonin Scalia, Clarence Thomas, and the author of the majority opinion in *Dobbs*, Samuel Alito) that certainty lies in the intention or meaning of the words in the Constitution as they existed at the time of its passage. Scalia, for example, said of his originalism that it ensured a "rock solid, unchanging Constitution" that, unlike the "living" Constitution propounded by others, led him to assert that the Constitution was "dead, dead, dead."[27] For these conservatives, as Edmund Morgan notes: "Though [the Constitution] is full of ambiguities designed to secure acceptance by different people who could read its provisions in different ways in different situations, it has to be treated the way Fundamentalists treat the Bible, as the utterance of a single mind with a single intent."[28] However, the fact that there was no singular meaning—even dictionaries of the era have multiple and divergent definitions, and the Founders' intentions were diverse and unrecoverable, as were those of legislators in ratifying states—that fact renders the originalists' arguments no less strategic than those of the liberals they criticize.[29] Indeed, rather than a quest for original meaning as such, for many judges it is arguably the need for certainty that is really the decisive factor. This is particularly true for a number of the Catholics on the highest court.

The presence of Catholics on the Supreme Court is not new. Among the fifteen Catholics who have served on the Court are Chief Justices Roger B. Taney and Edward Douglass White, as well as Associate Justices Pierce Butler, Joseph McKenna, Frank Murphy, and Sherman Minton (who converted to Catholicism after leaving the bench).[30] Currently there are six Catholics on the Court, including Sonia Sotomayor, who, like the former justices William Brennan and Anthony Kennedy, is a liberal Catholic, and Neil Gorsuch, raised Catholic but attending Episcopal services and whose attachments are not entirely clear. Whether their Catholicism affects their views on such key issues as abortion, the death penalty, and school prayer, the common denominator among the conservative Catholic justices and their academic backers would appear to be their need for certainty.[31] This need takes various forms.

The quest for certainty—a certainty based on precepts that stand outside and above any human creation—is integral to the message of the Catholic Church and thus to the many judges who cleave, if not to every one of its teachings, to the overall need for certainty it purports to provide in their lives. "He who doubts is damned," says Romans 14:23; as for "doubt as sin," writes Friedrich Nietzsche, "Christianity has done its utmost to close the circle and declared even doubt to be sin. One is supposed to be cast into belief without reason, by a miracle, and from then on to swim in it as in the brightest and least ambiguous of elements."[32] In his encyclical *Veritatis Splendor*, working from a draft sponsored by his counselor and successor, Cardinal Joseph Ratzinger (later Pope Benedict VII), Pope John Paul II taught that, no matter how separated someone is from God, "in the depths of his heart there always remains a yearning for absolute truth and a thirst to attain full knowledge of it."[33] Any hint of the equality of divergent moral codes, he said, is therefore to be condemned. Thus in the same encyclical the Pope blamed my own discipline, anthropology, for muddying the moral waters:

> [G]iving himself over to relativism and skepticism (cf. *John* 18:38), he [man] goes off in search of an illusory freedom apart from truth itself. . . . [A] new situation has come about *within the Christian community itself,* which has experienced the spread of numerous doubts and objections of a human and psychological, social and cultural, religious and even properly theological nature, with regard to the Church's moral teachings. It is no longer a matter of limited and occasional dissent, but of an overall and systematic calling into question of traditional moral doctrine, on the basis of certain anthropological and ethical presuppositions.[34]

This need for theological certainty clearly carries over into the current thinking of some Catholic jurists and legal scholars. Justice Scalia, for example, stressed that it is the role of a judge to do things "perfectly," which by definition means without any doubt or uncertainty, and attributed this orientation entirely to his Catholic faith.[35] And surely when he said that the point of the death penalty is not punishment or deterrence but "to set right the moral disorder that has been created by the crime," there is more than a modicum of re-creating certainty in such a proposition.[36] Another indicator of the need for certainty is the renewal of attachment to natural law. Although contemporary American courts have not recognized natural law as a source of law, Catholic jurists and legal scholars have grounded much of their current thinking on its claims.[37] Moreover, they have formed an alliance with Evangelicals—explicitly referred to as the "co-belligerency alliance"—in which abortion figures as a key connection. The confirmation hearings of Robert Bork for a place on the Supreme Court constituted an important moment in that movement. Bork was not, as many suppose, turned down primarily because of his originalist views about constitutional interpretation, rigid as they were, but for his demonstration to key senators, including many conservatives, that he was so certain about all issues that he would not possess the judicial temperament necessary to consider alternative arguments.[38] The combination of natural law, with its own claims to certainty, and an alliance with non-Catholics who form the core of conservativism in America, has contributed to a federal bench that rarely if ever bespeaks any doubt or cavil about its opinions. It has also led to a view of the Constitution that is equally certain and equally fixed.

Dobbs and other recent cases have exposed the tenuous basis of the broadly accepted view of constitutional interpretation that reasoned arguments, though widely variant, place limits on the personal, religious, and/or political decisions by judges. The question thus arises: Was that normative consensus a convenient myth, or was it as much as one can expect in a system that demands not conciliation but judgment? Some legal scholars are now forced to ask whether they had long been teaching constitutional law incorrectly if, in fact, that law has always been intensely politicized and is all but irretrievably so now.[39] They may, like one law professor, see the point of teaching constitutional law "not to come to any definitive answers but rather to introduce students to the idea of uncertainty and contingency in constitutional law."[40] Others fear that matters have gone too far. Legal commenter Dahlia Lithwick notes: "[W]e need at least the illusion of jurists capable of self-doubt. . . . But we are entering a Supreme Court era in which the Justices will largely operate free from doubt or intellectual humility or even meaningful interest in hearing opposing arguments."[41]

John Dewey once wrote: "Just because the personal element cannot be wholly excluded, while at the same time the decision must assume as nearly as possible an impersonal, objective, rational form, the temptation is to surrender the vital logic which has actually yielded the conclusion and to substitute for it forms of speech which are rigorous in appearance and which give an illusion of certitude."[42] Indeed, uncertainty is very personal, and if judgments are to appear oracular, removing the curtain to reveal the Wizard as a mere mortal risks undermining the claim to impersonal authority most contemporary legal systems crave. Indeed, the moment judges express uncertainty, their majority opinions may take on a personal identity (e.g., *Roe* becomes "the Blackmun decision," a crucial Indian fishing rights decision becomes "the [Judge] Boldt decision"[43]) subject to very different criteria of criticism than an opinion that hints at no uncertainty whatsoever. To some this transformation further undermines the court's legitimacy.

Doubt, however, does not have to lead to a loss of confidence in the outcome, to a pretense of certainty lest legitimacy be lost, or to the compromising of strongly held values.[44] It is true that doubt can lead to a form of gradualism, which Chief Justice Roberts was urging in *Dobbs* and to which courts have long paid respect. The result may be justice delayed—which need not be the same as justice denied—or it may mean that the past rules from the grave. But what is the alternative if the aim of the law cannot be shifted from determinate rulings to finding common ground? Even in the case of abortion that common ground clearly exists in popular sentiment: although all five majority votes in *Dobbs* were registered by Catholic justices, an overwhelming majority of Americans believe *some* situations warrant permitting abortion.[45] Only the Court's refusal to distinguish certitude from certainty, reservation from inaction, and compromise from solidarity can lead us to question whether such a middle course is possible. "'Does compromise always require something like splitting the difference?" asks Avishai Margalit. "Not quite. There is a notion that views the essence of compromise not so much in splitting the difference as in the willingness to accept a reconstruction of what is in dispute."[46]

Just as the legal scholar Karl Llewellyn once noted that there are a thousand ways of distinguishing away a precedent, so, too, there are innumerable ways in which the appearance of judicial certainty might be realistically ameliorated. Constitutional law scholars take diverse approaches, ranging from minimalists who would have the Court refuse many cases and decide others on a case-by-case restrictive basis, to maximalists who would have the Court state its propositions boldly and universally, to those who would have it both ways depending on the issue. The first seeks to limit uncertainty by holding a decision to a narrow fact situation, the second by asserting what must be done in all cases, the third, applying a sort of sliding scale, by limiting the bounds of certainty to so-called fulcrum cases and letting the indeterminacy of the law play itself out incrementally or through the acts of the legislator. In each instance, however, expressed doubt continues to be seen as a threat to the legitimacy of the process even when everyone knows that these transparent garments neither fit nor hide the emperor's nakedness.

So how to deal with uncertainty? The first thing to do is to recognize that uncertainty is not antithetical to legitimacy. Neither is doubt the opposite of certainty: As Tony Schwartz, who came to regret being the ghostwriter of *Trump: The Art of the Deal*, urges: "Let go of certainty. The opposite isn't uncertainty. It's openness, curiosity and a willingness to embrace paradox, rather than choose up sides." If American law is to proceed case by case—acknowledging that perfect resolution of larger issues raised by a given set of facts may have to await further instances—then that is hardly the same as giving in to uncertainty; rather it is to underscore that the common law system of reasoning is, to borrow Attorney General Edward Levi's characterization, a "moving system of categorizing concepts."[47] And "moving" is not the enemy of a working form of certainty.

Second, being Solomonic rather than absolute is sometimes both preferable and possible. It is not a matter of splitting the difference so that neither side gets what they desire but encouraging the best from all of those involved. In the case of abortion we could trust women to make the decision. We could do so not only in recognition of the individualistic nature of our culture but also because (as will be argued in chapter 3) the American Experiment in diversity demands that at some level—perhaps that of the highly personal—unity does indeed lie in diversity. If, for example, courts were to adopt the policy that the woman is trusted to make the decision until the very late stages of her pregnancy—and candidly cite Blackmun's memorandum to the effect that such a marker is based on uncertainty and an emphasis on the right to diversity in deeply personal matters—a more reasonable basis for further discussion might be possible for all but the most extreme proponents on either side. Such a stance will hardly satisfy the maximalists of the antiabortion movement, but it may be necessary to counter such absolutism in the name of preserving diversity and to claw our way back to some semblance of a shared middle course. Indeed, if the American ideal of community has any substance at all, any such attempt to reconstruct conversation would seem to be integral to employing that concept for a degree of reconciliation.

Moreover, acknowledgement of a degree of doubt, far from being antithetical to the goal of legal certainty, is fully in keeping with the common law's style of reasoning and its aims. The possession of some reservation indicates openness to change when knowledge and practice are themselves in flux, and it reaffirms that the decision in a case need not foreclose potential litigants finding new ways to accommodate their respective views. So, too, the concept of stare decisis can become at once a vehicle for the grounding of a legal precedent *and* an instrument for recognizing well-paced alterations. By augmenting respect for precedent with that other Latin concept—*quantum ad cognitionem*, or "to the best of our present understanding"—recognition is given to the paradigm shifts that may be in the offing. Indeed, Thomas Kuhn, in his analysis of such shifts, notes: "In science . . . a paradigm is rarely an object for replication. Instead, like an accepted judicial decision in the common law, it is an object for further articulation and specification under new or more stringent conditions."[48]

One way to finesse uncertainty, of course, is to avoid deciding cases where there is insufficient clarity as to how best to treat the matter. The buzz phrase here is "judicial restraint," a commitment every nominee to the Court pledges to honor. The problem, however, is that when those sitting on the Court have a majority or the public's ear they cannot resist reading the law as they wish, and when they are in the minority simply crying "restraint!" seldom produces it. Nevertheless, there are advantages to a period of restraint in a polarized environment. Such a pause would diminish the focus on court appointments as an election issue, discourage justices from acting like public celebrities, make it easier for the Court to allow televised broadcasts of their hearings, and afford a respite during which the Justices may re-create more common ground among themselves.

Judicial restraint, of course, is not without its disadvantages: A gridlocked Congress will not address vital issues, local controls may diminish national protections, minority rights may be jeopardized, and case-by-case selectivity may substitute for actual restraint. Like many proffered remedies, restraint may therefore be harsh in the taking and easily forgotten when the fever has broken. But once partisanship has been set in temporary abeyance it may be possible to build back shared criteria through cases of a less overtly political nature. The great power of the Court is its ability to capture the terms of discussion in such a way that those who disagree nevertheless engage in the conversation—conversation, again, being crucial to any sense of community. An enforced period of true restraint may be the best hope for resurrecting civil expressions of difference as a model for that self-same image of an imagined community.

Finally, judges could express their uncertainty over the larger application or principle in a case without damaging the decision on the facts before them. Admittedly, this is not an easy posture to maintain, neither if one is to appear to know what one is doing nor in a legal culture propelling us toward seemingly unambiguous answers. As journalist Margaret Talbot notes: "Ambivalence is a difficult state of mind to sustain; the temptation to replace it with a more Manichean vision is always close at hand." Worse yet, if it were true, is the claim that "ambivalence in the present moment is a condition worse than most because it can lead to catastrophe."[49] But owning up to less than absolute certainty could lead to more respect for alternative arguments, more nuanced sensitivity to context, and more realism in the way prospective members of the Court educate the public and the Senate in the course of the nominee's confirmation hearings.

"In both Plato and Job," wrote anthropologist Stanley Diamond, "it needs to be noted, the abolition of injustice depends on the obliteration of ambivalence, and the obliteration of ambivalence is the death of tragedy."[50] But are justice and ambivalence really at odds? Perhaps what we have lost, in life as in law, is the sense of tragedy, not in the sense that we are condemned by a fatal flaw or inherent sinfulness to a rueful end but the realization that the world is indeed a place of uncertainty and that, while granting each other a fair measure of leeway, we may only asymptotically approach absolute truth. Even judges may benefit from Aristotle's reminder: "It is the mark of an educated mind to rest satisfied with the degree of precision which the nature of the subject admits and not to seek exactness where only an approximation is possible." Lorraine Daston's distinction between those situations where one must attend to unique features, where judgment means reconciling universals and particulars, suggests a clear alternative to uncertainty and simple subjectivity.[51] So, too, the enhancement of a sense of community necessitates sufficient communication about the relation of the individual to the shared conceptualizations of society, a communication that emphasizes that the individual will not be lost in the generality. And if the ultimate goal is the preservation of conversation in a highly diversified community, then a fair recognition of uncertainty all around may not be inconsistent with the larger needs of such a collective endeavor.

Chief Justice Roberts is not alone in cautioning against too high a degree of certainty among his colleagues. In *Dobbs* he may be pleading, particularly with his conservative colleagues, to give some matters like abortion the benefit of the doubt and not, as now seems to be the case, only "the deficit of the doubt." He may have come to appreciate that a modicum of acknowledgment of uncertainty could only enhance the Court's legitimacy by humanizing its authoritative voice and reaffirming the crabwise mode of common law legal discourse. He may have recalled the admonition of Justice Oliver Wendell Holmes, Jr.: "Certitude is not the test of certainty. We have been cocksure of many things that were not so,"[52] or the admonition of the lawyer and congressman Frederic R. Coudert, who said "to make the law certain on subjects as to which the community itself is most uncertain . . . is a task that never has yet and never will be accomplished."[53] He might even have joined Judge Learned Hand in his observation that "the spirit of liberty is the spirit which is not too sure that it is right."[54] If, as Stanford Law School professor Pamela S. Karlan has said of the current composition of the Supreme Court, "this is a court that is very convinced of its righteousness,"[55] it may be all the more important—particularly for those justices who have a personal predilection for the absolute—to find a rhetoric that is at once clear as to the resolution of the case before them and appropriately honest in the recognition of its momentary and elusive certainty. If civil discourse is the lifeblood of community identity and cohesion a willingness to recognize that certitude is anathema to collective well-being, then it is essential for the utterances of the highest court to underscore that civility benefits, rather than suffers, when uncertainty is given its proper due.

3

Abortion and the Constitutional Protection of Diversity

At no point does the U.S. Constitution speak directly to the issue of individual or collective diversity. It does, of course, concentrate on states' rights, individual religious freedom, and the protection of alternative viewpoints. But it never addresses the safeguard of differentness as such, and in failing to do so it leaves open the question whether such assurance may nevertheless be found in the interstices of the Constitution's provisions.

The question, then, is whether an argument can be made, not unlike those on which other unenumerated rights have been based, for the protection of a personal and collective right to diversity, a right that would seem to be not only consonant with but integral to the very idea of the United States as a multicultural society. Indeed, could such a right be integral to a range of protectible practices including laws relating to education, housing, and even abortion? Given the explicit reference in numerous legal decisions to the importance placed on diversity without discrimination, perhaps it is time to consider whether an extended reading of the Constitution needs to catch up with the changing emphases in American culture. In doing so we might also have an opportunity to consider just what the protection of diversity means to the ongoing American romance of community.

* * *

The reversal of *Roe v. Wade* by the Supreme Court in *Dobbs v. Jackson Women's Health Organization* sends the issue of abortion back to the states and possibly Congress.[1] *Dobbs* does not, therefore, mean that constitutional litigation on the issue is at an end.[2] The question thus persists: On what constitutional basis may we ground a recognition of limited state involvement in so personal a decision as that of abortion? While many of the well-known arguments will be resurrected in the post-*Dobbs* era, this question may still be susceptible to new forms of constitutional interpretation, especially as it concerns the place of diversity in our constitutional scheme.

In the past, judicial decisions and legal commentary on abortion and related matters have centered on the Equal Protection Clause of the Fourteenth Amendment and the right of privacy said to be integral, if unstated, to the fulfilment of established rights. But one possibility that has not been fully considered concerns the Ninth Amendment of the Constitution, which states: "The enumeration in the Constitution, of certain rights, shall not be construed to deny or disparage others retained by the people." Theories of the amendment's meaning and scope are quite varied, and much, therefore, rides on which interpretation one favors.[3]

To some commenters and judges, the authors and ratifiers of the Constitution intended the amendment as protection for those rights not otherwise enumerated; to others it has been seen as preserving states' rights, as protecting rights recognized in the common law, as a hedge against laws that might limit one's rights, as the preservation of an individual's "natural" rights, or as a vehicle for reserving the collective right of the people to change its form of government.[4] Members of the Supreme Court have also held widely divergent views: Justice Robert H. Jackson characterized the Ninth Amendment as a "mystery,"[5] Justice Arthur Goldberg argued that it forms the basis for a right to privacy, and Justice Potter Stewart maintained that the amendment cannot be used to limit the right of states to pass laws affecting their citizens.[6] Nevertheless, as one legal scholar states: "I know of not a single figure from the Founding who asserted clearly that enumerated rights would or did hold an enhanced legal status that unenumerated rights lacked."[7] While it is true that the courts have not turned to the Ninth Amendment in the same way they have relied on broad interpretations of other amendments in the Constitution, the issue has not been carefully explored in recent years.[8]

If, then, one sees constitutional interpretation not as bound to a rigidly originalist view—and if one casts the Ninth Amendment in the broader context of the nation's foundational design and purpose—it could be argued that the whole point of the American Experiment is to achieve diversity within unity and that the Ninth Amendment plays a central role in furthering that end. George Washington, in his "Farewell Address," could tell his countrymen: "With slight shades of difference, you have the same religion, manners, habits, and political principles."[9]

But his touchstone—the belief that regional differences were overborn by shared nationhood, gender, and class and that the real danger lay in factional politics—focused attention on differences among the states rather than among individuals or cultural groups. "Here is not a nation," said Walt Whitman, "but a nation of nations." Nevertheless, unity in *personal* diversity—rather than unity through uniformity or category identity—was vital to the new nation. The national motto—which derives from Cicero's paraphrase of Pythagoras: "When each person loves the other as much as himself, it makes one out of many (*unum fiat ex pluribus*)"[10]—emphasizes the individual and is accompanied by a prohibition on state-sponsored religion while preserving the diversity of personal faith within the various states. During the past decade, businesses and universities have revitalized the idea of cultural variation through guidelines aimed at "diversity, equity, and inclusion." The commitment to national identity through national diversity can have no legal support if one does not recognize that the Ninth Amendment preservation of diversity is no less vital to the recognition of penumbral rights as similar interpretations the courts have asserted.

The problem, then, is one of balancing the diverse with the unified and determining which units—the individual, the community, or both—should figure prominently in the analysis. It is not only unity that figures conspicuously in American law. The preservation—if not, indeed, the encouragement—of diversity through the law is more common than might be imagined: it is at the heart of many national laws and international agreements. In the United States, the Native American Graves Protection Act[11] and the Supreme Court decisions addressing the consideration of background in university admissions underscores the current emphasis on diversity as a fundamental concern. During oral argument in the Harvard and University of North Carolina affirmative action cases, both Solicitor General Elizabeth Prelogar and several justices emphasized that diversity was essential to innovation, the reduction of stereotypes, and—through the Reserve Officer Training Corps program—ensuring that military leadership roles reflect the diversity of enlisted service members.[12] The banning of books from public libraries that concern gay and transgender people may also be seen not only as an issue of gender discrimination but also as an attack on the right of "the people" to the preservation of diversity.[13] So, too, common law developments in the fields of defamation, parental rights, and the wearing of religious symbols—along, for example, with executive orders relating to diversity in the award of government contracts—may also be seen, in part, as bulwarks against uniformity. Indeed, it was in recognition of such diversity in an earlier gay rights case that Justice Harry Blackmun, joined in his dissent by Justices William Brennan, Thurgood Marshall, and John Paul Stevens, wrote: "Disapproval of homosexuality cannot justify invading the houses, hearts and minds of citizens who choose to live their lives differently."[14] Similarly, on the international level, the Convention on Biological Diversity,[15] UNESCO Recommendation on the Safeguarding of Traditional Culture and Folklore,[16] International Labor Organization Indigenous and Tribal Peoples Convention, 1989 (No. 169),[17] and Universal Declaration on Cultural Diversity[18] all have as their purpose the protection of a range of lifeways, not just their equal treatment under the law.[19]

But where in the Constitution is one to find protection for this diversity? The Ninth Amendment, which does not mention the states, clearly suggests that diversity is an attribute of groups and individuals; the Tenth explicitly mentions the states, and like the Ninth it adds "or the people." While both the Ninth and Tenth Amendments have been interpreted as primarily about states, reference in both to "the people" highlights the national need for diversity's creative and adaptive force and individuals' need for the protection of diversity as they operate in a world that is not, in fact, uniform.[20]

There are, of course, dangers attendant on deferring to "the people" as to any power. States, claiming to speak in the name of the people, may, as they have in the past, seek to nullify federal laws, while concern for some deeper law of the folk may institutionalize local discrimination—and suddenly the advantages of national unity unravel. Presumably, the courts, at whatever level, can ameliorate the worst aspects of local law by weighing them against constitutional protections. Diversity may, therefore, be a starting point rather than a catchall residual requirement, its emphasis and the developing case law having beneficial implications that may not seem immediately obvious.

Indeed, it may be argued, something more flows from the proposition that diversity must be protected in the nation's multicultural experiment, for what is vital to each of the statutory, case law, and historical examples cited is that we trust the affected members of our nation to be able to choose—many would add "to flourish"—among those diverse aspects of their personhood that government action should not undermine. If the right to privacy—much less "liberty" or "happiness"—means anything, it could well be seen to incorporate the protection of individual and collective diversity. The Supreme Court might, therefore, stay closer to the Constitution if it recognized that the collective right to diversity is integral to the Ninth Amendment and that such diversity cannot itself be fulfilled without trusting each citizen to make the most intimate and sensitive decisions affecting their personal lives. Moreover, as in the case of barring segregation, individuals are entitled not to have their differences from the majority brought into public disrespect or their self-regard diminished.[21] The term "disparage" in the Ninth Amendment—meaning "to treat as being of little worth"—is no less applicable when we trust our citizens to make the most personal of their life decisions.

Like the other examples cited, in the case of abortion the argument can then be made that the goal of diversity is furthered by trusting women to make their own decisions. This is not the same as situations where a crime is involved, although it may at times mean having to pay a price in order to sustain the advantages of diversity. And it is not the same as a case in which women are being treated differently than men in their pay or advancement, cases in which the issue is more appropriately analyzed in terms of equal protection or due process. Rather, "the people" have both a collective and a personal interest in the protection of diversity if the American Experiment is to hold any meaning and chance of success.

Diversity might also be said to connect with the concept of dignity, defined here in its legal rather than strictly moral valence. The contemporary idea of dignity in law is largely associated with the jurisprudence of former justice Anthony Kennedy.[22] While he may have been influenced by the declarations on dignity by Pope John XXIII, as in his 1963 encyclical *Pacem In Terris*,[23] Kennedy's own argument was no less grounded in an interpretation of the underlying implications of the Constitution than in a literal reading of that document.[24] In his use of the concept of dignity, Kennedy also echoes the language of the Ninth Amendment when, borrowing the word "disparage," he states: "The federal statute is invalid, for no legitimate purpose overcomes the purpose and effect to disparage and injure those whom the state, by its marriage laws, sought to protect in personhood and dignity."[25] Others coming at matters from a different orientation have also shared in Kennedy's usage: Justice Brennan, a liberal Catholic, used the word "dignity" thirty-five times in his well-known speech at Georgetown University in 1985.[26] Dignity, like privacy, may, of course, reside in the eye of the beholder, its relationship to diversity being more a matter of one's jurisprudential philosophy than strict construction. But to the extent that one does indeed see the Constitution as a living document, the combination of these two concepts—rather like the elision of due process and equal protection—offers an interpretation that seeks to enhance the balance between individual rights and state powers.

The protection of true diversity may also be the most appropriate antidote to exaggerated protection of distinctiveness, those forms of wokeness and cancel culture that lead individuals to find fault with any act or utterance they regard as offensive. This may include, but not be limited to, the showing of an artistic rendering of the Prophet Muhammad that some Muslim students may find offensive or the classroom explication of a text that incorporates a racial epithet.[27] But genuine diversity recognizes that groups are themselves not uniform. As one commentor notes: "Too many people today demand that we respect the diversity of society, but fail to see the diversity of minority communities within those societies. As a result, progressive voices often get dismissed as not being authentic, while the most conservative figures become celebrated as the true embodiment of their communities."[28] Thus an emphasis on diversity, as envisioned in the Ninth Amendment, may become a vital instrument for preserving intragroup variation just as it may promote intergroup respect.

Dignity, diversity, personhood—each is a contestable concept, yet each echoes the risk we have chosen to take in constructing a nation based on difference. In telling phrases that resonate with respect for this diversity, the Quran says: "If we had chosen we could have made you all the same"; a Hebrew prayer thanks God for creating "many souls and their deficiencies" so each must complement what the other lacks; and Pope Francis could assert that "[d]iplomacy is called to be truly inclusive, not canceling but cherishing the differences and sensibilities that have historically marked various peoples."[29] Free-market "theology" makes the same argument: God wishes "human friendships to be engendered by mutual needs and resources," said the Dutch political philosopher and lawyer Hugo Grotius, "lest individuals deeming themselves entirely sufficient unto themselves should for that very reason be rendered unsociable."[30] It is precisely in variation, too, that evolution works its wonders, that individuals attend to each other and express their most human of categorizing capacities, and that a nation demonstrates whether it trusts all its people or only the few who claim to know best. It is a test the United States will continue to face not only in the abortion debate but in many issues that touch on the personal choices we must all make in life and the impact those choices have on our sense of community.

4

Group Defamation

Can groups be defamed or only individuals? In the United States the answer is: only individuals. In many other countries, however, group defamation is indeed actionable. Is it a difference of history that accounts for such alternative approaches, or of philosophy, concepts of the person, or the politics of the moment? Is injury to a specific individual the same as an injury spread over an entire category of persons? Indeed, what exactly is the rationale for allowing any suit for personal defamation, particularly in an age of woke sensibility and cancel culture? Do such lawsuits interfere with freedom of speech? Though hurtful to the average person's sensibilities, if there is no actual loss of position, resources, or safety, does the balance of concerns weigh more favorably for or against allowing such speech? Or is injurious speech really an act, and not a mere utterance, such that the idea of "sticks and stones will break my bones but names will never hurt me" should not be the legal standard? Indeed, who actually represents the affected group? And what, exactly, are the appropriate remedies?

In this chapter we will not review all the world's approaches to group defamation or every rationale that has been proffered in favor of its legal enforceability. Rather, concentrating on the American context, we will review the key arguments for and against institutionalizing such a cause of action and consider, in particular, whether changing cultural norms necessitate new legal protections or whether restraining their application except where clear bodily or financial harm can be shown has the salutary effect of requiring citizens to address such problems through new methods of resolution.

* * *

Just as the defamation of a single person may injure one's capacity to garner the trust needed to interact with others, so utterances and publications that bring an entire group into disrepute may affect the style of peaceful engagement among a society's constituent units. At the level of collective libel, however, distinctive legal and political issues arise. Shall freedom of speech preclude or protect such communications? Must one show that the statements were intended to incite harmful conduct or is it sufficient to demonstrate that they tend toward that effect? Must actual harm be proved, whether to identifiable persons or even a small category of people? If so, should the remedy be civil or criminal? If the harm is conceptualized as individual rather than collective, should only an affected person have standing to bring a suit? And even if enforcement is rare, does it beneficially affect public morals and discourse to designate such behavior as illegal?

Though long of concern, group defamation came to legal prominence mainly after the events of World War II.[1] Encounters with ethnic genocide were coupled with the emphasis on human rights to produce various international accords. Article 4 of the Convention on the Elimination of All Forms of Racial Discrimination proscribes the dissemination of racist materials and incitement to racial hatred and discrimination; Article 20 of the Covenant on Civil and Political Rights condemns incitement to national and religious hostility or violence; several UN resolutions prohibit the defamation of religions;[2] and other declarations promulgated by UNESCO have similarly proscribed discriminatory propaganda. However, a number of countries, including the United States, have entered reservations to these treaties, arguing, for example, that their own statutes protect free speech without these conventions' overreach. Regardless, at the international level enforcement of conventions and resolutions has proven difficult if not impossible to implement.

At the national and local levels, statutes have also had limited success. It was only in 2008 that the United Kingdom abolished penalties for blasphemy of the Christian religion, though Northern Ireland still retains such laws. In the United States, several states first adopted then repealed group libel laws or extended existing criminal statutes, and courts declared some formulations unconstitutional. Building on Supreme Court standards, the debate has often focused on whether some "clear and present danger" must be shown or whether intent is a necessary element of an unprotected utterance. The 1947 *Columbia Law Review* model statute embraces a strict-liability provision, while others would require at least a showing of recklessness or negligence.[3] Unlike private defamation, many statutes have emphasized public prosecution rather than leaving matters to individual suit. Case law has upheld some actions combating the use of racial epithets or insulting names, but the Supreme Court, in *R.A.V. v. St. Paul*, disallowed prosecutions for cross-burning where the statute was aimed mainly at the content of the speech rather than endangerment.[4]

Since each country has its own history of intergroup animosity, approaches to group defamation also vary. In Great Britain, for example, personal defamation has long been comparatively easy to establish, truth being essentially the only defense. Thus, in what was effectively a group defamation action involving a suit by a Holocaust denier against an author he claimed libeled him, the issue was joined indirectly rather than through the application of the Race Relations and Public Order Acts.[5] The result, as in all such litigation, has the social effect of disseminating the libel still further through the surrounding publicity, but this may have the salutary effect of articulating collective standards of civility and public discourse. It has been argued as well that refusal to restrict group libel ensures a greater flow of information, devalues the search for common standards of truth, grants power to purveyors of stereotypes, or demonstrates that "the avoidance of bad behavior toward bad behavior can be a value." The relative effectiveness of group defamation statutes remains uncertain, but their role in countries with a long history of virulent group hatred no doubt accounts for their differential rationales and adoption.

Other countries, other approaches.[6] Specific statutes include the Canadian Criminal Code's emphasis on incitement to racial hatred "likely to lead to a breach of the peace"; the Indian Penal Code's focus on words that promote "disharmony or feelings of enmity, hatred or ill-will" among groups; certain laws in France, Denmark, and Germany that require no showing of intent and punish denial of genocide (Armenian, for example, as well as Nazi); and the Israeli laws criminalizing even unsuccessful attempts "with the purpose of stirring up racism" and the denial of reelection to the Knesset to any party that seeks to "incite to racism." The implementation of these statutes is not, of course, self-executing, and their course depends on the overall scope and shape of judicial power in each situation. However, there is some evidence to suggest that they work best when combined with other antidiscrimination practices (as in Europe and the United Kingdom) and are least effective when turned against particular minority populations (as in Sri Lanka and South Africa).

In the United States, group defamation has found consideration at universities through the adoption of various hate-speech codes. However, these codes have been repeatedly struck down by courts who see them as vague and either over- or underinclusive.[7] Whenever my own students have attempted to write a campus hate-speech code they have come up against the common problem of either making the rules so broad that they are unclear as to what is covered or so detailed as to fail to incorporate everything reprehensible. Moreover, as in society at large, if a student were to question, say, biological claims for racial inequality or the prevalence of criminal characteristics among a certain population, or employ a term that is subjectively offensive to some members of a group, there is no broad legal agreement as to whether the case should be decided on the basis of the content or the potential effect of the utterance.

In general, American law does not allow civil suits for group defamation unless the group is so small that an individual could be readily identified by reference to the group. *The Restatement (Second) of Torts* codifies this approach: "One who publishes defamatory matter concerning a group or class of persons is subject to liability to an individual member of it if, but only if, the group or class is so small that the matter can reasonably be understood to refer to the member, or the circumstances of publication reasonably give rise to the conclusion that there is particular reference to the member."[8] In an attempt to maintain the central concept of defamation as personal injury, some courts have tried to limit the size of the group involved to twenty-five persons, while several states (including Oklahoma and New York), while acknowledging the general import of group size without specifying a limit, stress whether the intensity of suspicion cast on the plaintiff is factually supportable.[9] Moreover, given forms and levels of proof drawn historically from other legal causes of action, proving group defamation, even where the size requirement is met, can be extremely difficult. As one commenter noted: "The difficulties faced by the group defamation victim are obvious on paper and terrifying in reality. In merely defending his reputation, he is confronted by unprovable issues and . . . is bludgeoned in court by a history of 'rational reasonable' civil and criminal precedents."[10] Given inconsistent results, vague criteria, and continuing worries over limitations on free speech, to say that the approaches of the past have achieved their own professed goals would be at best an exaggeration.[11]

Indeed, many commenters argue that free speech must tolerate some abuses and that the most effective way to combat any form of injurious misinformation is by subjecting it to the sterilizing light of public debate. Where reasoned discussion is not possible, however, such an approach is, in the eyes of a number of commenters, largely illusory.[12] To some, trying to find a perfect group defamation law is also a feckless pursuit.[13] But if establishing a statutory framework has proven largely untenable, attention might be shifted from the emphasis on the individual litigator to the concept of the individual as embedded—but not necessarily submerged—in a broader community. In this regard, the sometimes contradictory American romance of community and the emphasis on the individual need to be brought into greater focus.

That American courts should emphasize the role of the individual rather than any group in defamation cases is hardly surprising: American culture has long placed primary emphasis on the individual; the law, which recognizes the state and the individual as legal entities, gives little notice to groups or communities that cannot be easily analogized with either of the two superordinate categories.[14] This leaves almost no room for collectivities, however much the individual members identify themselves or are identified by others in terms of some common feature or association, with any legal remedy for the injury they may suffer. Thus a number of dilemmas remain unaddressed.[15] What standards should be implemented to determine offensive or inciting utterances? Is the criterion to be simply subjective, or is some standard of reasonable offensiveness to be applied? Who speaks for the group claiming libel, particularly since no group is itself entirely uniform? What is a sufficient level of offense to trigger a hearing or remedy: Are dog whistles sufficient, or must the libel be so explicit as to be immediately recognizable by all? If many utterances have some truth in them, what percentage of falsehood will suffice for action? If remedies afforded are minimal, what broader harm to attitudes and relations may be done that could have been prevented? And if significant remedies are to be sought, are formal courts of law necessarily the best instrument for the purpose?

To many legal analysts, defamation law generally, and group defamation laws particularly, are so often inconsistently applied that their criteria and outcomes lack genuine clarity and predictability.[16] So the question arises whether the problem is less one of the laws to be applied than whether there is some fault in the process itself. Might not some other forum, some other set of procedures and remedies, some other set of presumptions and burdens be given consideration? If, as H. L. A. Hart noted, the law faces the twinned problems of uncertainty of fact and indeterminacy of aim, perhaps we need to start with each of these problems and then make the process fit the purpose rather than assume that rules of procedure developed for general courts of law are necessarily appropriate to the group defamation problem. Toward that end we might consider several alternative fora.

Much has been said about alternative dispute resolution (ADR) mechanisms in the United States and elsewhere. In the 1980s former Chief Justice Warren Burger told his profession:

> Our system is too costly, too painful, too destructive, too inefficient for a truly civilized people. To rely on the adversary process as the principal means of resolving conflicting claims is a mistake that must be corrected. . . . The entire legal profession—lawyers, judges, law teachers—has become so mesmerized with the stimulation of the courtroom contest that we tend to forget that we ought to be healers—healers of conflicts.[17]

Though numerous models of ADR have been tried—from local community courts to workplace fora to mediation overseen by courts, religious organizations, or professional societies—matching a mechanism to a culture to ensure adequate legitimacy is not easy to fashion ab initio. In hearings about legislation mandating the formation of alternative mechanisms, Congress itself noted the success of such fora as the Kpelle Moot of West Africa and the Native American Peacemaker courts, while the Jewish Conciliation Board of New York, Florida's rent-a-retired-judge program, and the mediation mechanisms employed by diamond and grain merchants all suggest alternative modes of addressing disputes. Perhaps, for reasons both of legitimacy and consistency, the most appropriate format in the United States to hear group defamation claims would be the establishment of special venues capable of developing many of their own procedures and case law, venues that would nevertheless be partially integrated with existing courts—much in the way that divorce and other family law mechanisms are often employed. Toward that end a hybrid format might be suggested that draws on several models, including that of the Indian Claims Commission (ICC), various community courts, the ADR Act, and the experience of truth and reconciliation commissions.[18]

In 1946 the United States Congress established the Indian Claims Commission as a vehicle for addressing all outstanding claims by Native Americans against the federal government. The Commission could award monetary damages but no land. Its mandate allowed even moral claims against the United States, though the underlying aim of the law was to settle all possible suits and then terminate the special status of the tribes. However, the Commission took its mandate seriously and added its own interpretations. Not only did it allow moral claims; it consistently refused to offset the awards with the value of goods the federal government had "given" the tribes as part of various treaty accords, a refusal that eventuated in Congress backing down from the requirement. Operating as what might be seen as the last great common law court, the Commission developed its own procedures, allowing considerable scope for relevant evidence and encouraging a wide view of the history of tribal-federal relations. From this experience several features might be transferable to the group defamation situation.

First, the lesson of the ICC is to open the bounds of relevance quite widely. Thus, in the case of group defamation, a broad understanding of context, history, and innuendo should be within the compass of the hearing. Second, it should be understood that, while the goal is not the application of a single moral code, there is a moral valence to the proceedings, and that one aspect of the process is to help effectuate a collective sense of moral limits and moral possibilities that attend on group defamation claims. Finally, while direct punishment would not be part of the forum's mandate (any more than the ICC could award land), it can offer the opportunity to be heard and for findings to be made known that are so essential to a collective sense of acceptable forms of speech.

From the Jewish Conciliation Board and similar community fora, one may take several additional lessons. First, it has often been demonstrated that, while a favorable result is obviously sought by any plaintiff, the goal is often less a matter of obtaining victory than it is about having one's day in court, about having one's felt sense of injury publicly attended to. We know, for example, that small-claims courts or television courts (*The People's Court, Judge Judy*, etc.) appeal to participants mainly because someone is listening to their grievance. So, too, group defamation hearings should not only be open to the public; they should recognize that even though the forum's remedies may be limited the greater remedy—public attendance to hurt and public acknowledgment of appropriate standards of civility in public discourse—is worthy of collective support. Indeed, it may be best to call the forum the Group Defamation Board, rather than by the name of a court, to underscore that it employs a very broad process and is not governed solely by the rules of courts of general jurisdiction.

The ADR requires each federal court to establish alternative mechanisms for the handling of disputes. One of the main ways this can be accomplished under the legislation is with community involvement. While different districts might choose different formats (as under the ADR Act), some form of community representation on the Group Defamation Board may be advisable. Although the ADR Act specifies the use of a panel of "neutrals" who (the statute says) "*should* be trained" for the task of mediation or arbitration, the Board need not necessarily require professional training, just as it is not required of ordinary jurors.[19] Whether it is clergy or respected citizens, a mixed panel of professional and nonprofessional members can add both to legitimacy and spreading the word as to what is and is not acceptable speech about a group. Just as juries are employed in common law countries and mixed panels of judges and laypersons in Continental systems of law, so, too, in the case of a forum set up under the aegis of the courts to hear these cases, a localized form of community involvement may offer the greatest chance for overall success. Unlike the ADR Act, local federal court rules keep matters confidential and require litigants to pay costs of the proceedings, whereas the forum suggested here is necessarily public and should not be a financial burden to the parties.

Truth and reconciliation commissions have been set up in a number of countries with a wide range of historical backdrops. Instances include those concerned with the treatment of First Nation students in Canada, the "Days of Lead" under the late King Hassan of Morocco, and most famously the commission in South Africa following the end of apartheid. Such commissions are also not unknown in the United States.[20] By not meting out punishments to those who are forthright in their acknowledgment of past deeds, the commissions have at least made public much of what was suspected but not acknowledged and invoked the moral authority of their process to grant some comfort to the affected. A group defamation process may benefit from a similar ethos and the utilization of some of the techniques that proved most effective in these proceedings. Once again, it is local history, local personnel, and local publicity that may have to be taken into consideration in each instance, as the racial buzzwords or sensibilities of one region may not be identical to that of another.

Given these factors, a proposal for legislative enactment might incorporate the following terms:

The Group Defamation Act

1. In a suit alleging group defamation the Court shall determine:
   a. that the content of the utterance or publication on its face constitutes or portents actual harm to the reputation or well-being of those maligned, whether individually, as a small group, or as members of a distinguishable category;
   b. that the communication has occurred more than once, whether in the same or closely similar form, such as to constitute a course of conduct or pattern; and
   c. that even if not explicit and not otherwise protected under existing First Amendment law a reasonable person may pierce the veil of indirection to understand what is its clear meaning and about whom the communication is directed.
2. Given a finding of probable cause of group defamation the matter shall be assigned to the Group Defamation Board. The Board shall have the power:
   a. to subpoena the defendant and other involved parties;
   b. to hear from expert witnesses, members of the community affected, and any other witnesses the Board may deem capable of assisting in its assessment of the charges;
   c. to render an opinion as to whether the allegation of group defamation is supported by the evidence;

d. to hold its hearings in public and, in any finding of group defamation, to make public the names and organizations of those found guilty;

e. to recommend to the supervising court that they place a party found guilty of group defamation on probation, any violation of which shall trigger a hearing for contempt of court, the punishments being those normally allocated to such a finding; and

f. to invite those found guilty to meet with their accusers to consider a way to avoid such suits in the future.

Several aspects of this proposal warrant further comment.

Combating group defamation through law or lawlike mechanisms may depend for their success to some degree on the form of publicity afforded their process and findings. A jury trial may evoke public sentiment, but other forms of community involvement may be more effective. The proposal above foresees court oversight of the Board's proceedings, as it does divorce mediation, and incorporates methods that are more responsive to the situation than are ordinary criminal and civil suits, as it does in juvenile and family proceedings. Having community members take a public stand renders the criteria for acceptable speech more visible. If punishment as such is not the goal but public opprobrium, what matters is the articulation of what we are willing as a community to regard as factually supportable and acceptable to a shared sense of civility.

The laws of defamation in the United States require a showing of actual, present harm, not speculative future harm. This proposed statute recognizes that current defamatory speech *is* current harm, that speech is an act with immediate consequences, particularly if it perpetuates a false and malicious view of a category of citizenry who have every right to remain free from threat. The requirement that the defamatory speech not be a one-off event protects against the off-chance remark, and it affords an opportunity for it to be retracted or regretted. But if a pattern can be shown, despite variation, probable cause may be found, which initiates a process whose goal is truth and for which reconciliation would be a plus.

There will be, of course, outstanding issues: How extensive may the Board couch its decision as it concerns the public shaming of a guilty party? What if any appeal ought to be allowed following a Board decision? Will courts be overwhelmed with those seeking attention for their felt sense of injury? Will others purposely seek to offend in order to air their grievances with the affected in a more public setting—one that will have very limited penalties attached? Or will the effect be to cancel legitimate criticism of groups lest one be brought up on group defamation charges?

To these and similar reservations there can only be one answer: Until one tries, one does not know for sure.[21] But courts can dismiss frivolous suits quickly, establish a level of probable cause as experience develops, and—like other such fora we have mentioned—bring issues to light more usefully than under existing defamation proceedings. The proposed statute also brings the community and the local culture more fully into the proceedings, not only by its openness to a wide range of evidence but also by its localization and attention to the history of meanings in that context. Ultimately, this is a process in which speech *is* confronted by more speech, with all parties placed in a neutral forum where that truth may have an opportunity to emerge and be legitimized. In the realm of group defamation—where the harm cannot be remedied under the guise of unlimited free speech—a forum that gains legitimacy as it gains in the exposure of falsehood is well worth the indeterminacies that may still have to be addressed.

PART II

Enabling Vulnerable Communities

5

Adjudicating the Disposition of Indigenous Remains

The Case for Special Forums

Justice Oliver Wendell Holmes, Jr., famously said that "jurisdiction is power": to force someone into your courts, to subject them to your laws, to enjoin or fine or incarcerate someone is surely a power of enormous import. The choice of venue, then, no less than the rules to be applied, is crucial, and how one goes about constructing the most appropriate forum for a given category of disputes tests both the goal to be sought and the remedies that may facilitate that end. This is no less the case when the issue is one of determining control of the bodies of indigenous peoples.

Customs relating to the disposition of their kinsmen's remains have varied quite widely in Native North America. So, too, the law has been in flux, particularly since the recognition that identifiable remains ought, in certain circumstances, to be repatriated to the tribe with which they are most clearly identified. But while recent laws and the practices of museums, collectors, and academics have changed, potential disputes still go before state or federal courts of general jurisdiction. The issue raised in this chapter concerns whether, in an age of DNA testing and greater sensitivity to native concerns, more specialized courts ought to be formed to address such cases. If one aspect of relations with Native Americans is the strengthening of their communities, and if the return of their ancestors' remains is vital to their sense of collective well-being, issues of bodily integrity and the disposition of human remains are vitally important. Who decides this, and how such forums are constituted, are indispensable issues to the pursuit of fairness to all parties.

* * *

In nearly every culture—and particularly in every religion—there is some promise of personal life after death. It is often necessary, therefore, to connect one's mortal remains with after-existence, whether by freeing the soul from its worldly dwelling or preparing those remains for their later state. Death rites may mirror the social role of the deceased, the threat and promise to society of their departure, and the shifting concepts of transition itself. The meaning attributed to such preparations and the forms they take thus mirror much of the society they serve and often carry, through the intensity of their attendant emotions, the ideas upon which a culture depends when death threatens the very order of things.

The disposition of the dead varies enormously. In the case of American Indians, those forms are as varied as the organization of the groups themselves. For many ancient groupings (ca. 1000–200 BCE), as seen particularly in the eastern United States, elaborate burial mounds probably replicated the social order of settlements or the vision of the cosmos at large; for others, like the Choctaw, Plains Indians, or Northwest Coast tribes, the spirits of the dead could be released only by first exposing them to the elements, the scattered remains sometimes being subject to secondary interment; for still others, as among a number of groups in the Southeast, the dead were placed in large earthenware jars before burial. Tribes of the Great Lakes region employed collective "Feast of the Dead" reburial ceremonies when engaging new groups in negotiated alliances.[1] As many Indians and Aleuts were converted to Christianity by Hispanics, Europeans, or Russians, burial in cemeteries, with appropriate religious insignia, became far more common. To the extent that one can generalize, for Native Americans locale and cosmos came together in the rituals of daily life including, with special force, the treatment of the place with which the remains of one's predecessors were associated.

Just as white Americans will go to extravagant lengths to recover the bodies of their dead or to visit the place where they died, so, too, for Native Americans deprivation of their dead has been felt with special intensity. The forced removal of Indians from the East, the creation of circumscribed reservations, and the loss of Indian lands exacerbated the sense of separation from ancestors. Throughout the Indian wars of the nineteenth century, the remains of fallen Indians were collected by the United States Army, the bodies being stripped of their flesh and the bones sent back to Washington. Housed for decades in government and private institutions, thousands of skulls and bones were hidden away or subjected to every passing scientific notion—from the relation of cranial size to intelligence, to the development of civilization as determined by denture, diet, or DNA. Often, too, the remains were placed on view in public or private museums, commonly with unflattering labels or surroundings. To Indians, these collections and exhibits, whether for science or for profit, were nothing short of the desecration to which, they argued, non-Indian remains were never subjected.

Many of these issues came to a head in the 1970s and 1980s, when Indian legal groups filed lawsuits seeking the discontinuance of offensive displays and the return of Indian remains. There was, however, no clear legal right to the return of such remains—whether the 18,500 sets of remains in the Smithsonian Institution or the hundreds of skeletons plundered in the late 1980s from a site in Kentucky. In 1990, therefore, the United States Congress passed the Native American Graves Protection and Repatriation Act (NAGPRA), which explicitly classifies human remains as "cultural items" that could be returned to related successor tribes.[2] As museum and university inventories were constructed and tribes asserted the right of return, archaeologists and native groups sometimes came into conflict: Most native peoples object to any scientific studies of their ancestors' remains, while scholars often asserted the benefits of allowing their studies to go forward. Several states (including California) also passed statutes or entered into agreements with tribes allowing the return of burial remains even from private sites. Further federal protection criminalizing the illegal excavation or trafficking in human remains was afforded by the Archaeological Resources Protection Act of 1978. Tribes themselves have also adopted codes affecting archaeological work on their reservations, and some have even sought to make their laws extend to remains housed beyond Indian lands. Several international human rights conventions have also proven an effective basis for the return of remains to peoples of the South Pacific, but since the United States is not a signatory to some of these treaties international standards have yet to be applied to Native Americans.

Perhaps the most difficult issue has been the question of ancient remains. When a set of 8,000–9,000-year-old bones, known as Kennewick Man, was discovered in Washington State, the Army Corps of Engineers sought to transfer the bones to the five tribes who claimed a connection to them.[3] In 2004 the U.S. Court of Appeals for the Ninth Circuit held that the requirement that there be some relation of the remains to an existing tribe, people, or culture had not been met in this case, and the court permitted scientists to gain access to the materials.[4] Other cases may also test the meaning of "indigenous" and the criteria for showing "cultural affiliation," key terms that are not clearly defined in the statutes themselves.[5] Nevertheless, where historical connections can be asserted, the capacity of tribes to regain control over their people's burial remains has significantly increased since the 1980s.

The human remains issue is but another example of America's deep-seated ambivalence toward native peoples. From the restraints that Chief Justice John Marshall (1755–1835) sought to place on the federal government's care of its "domestic dependent nations" to the willingness of white Americans who would never adopt a black child but would readily accept an Indian into their families, the course of American history has never been a simple story. The question of science versus heritage, identity versus property, thus replicates much of white-Indian relations and the ambivalence with which each approaches the actions and intentions of the other. The idea that Indians are like the miner's canary—that they give an early indication of the quality of the environs in which everyone operates—is no less true where archaeological remains are concerned than where land, natural resources, or the constitutional limits of indigenous sovereignty are also at issue.

The problem continues to be quite extensive. Notwithstanding the return of large numbers of Native American remains in the thirty years between 1990 and 2020, the Government Accounting Office estimates that some 116,000 remains continue to be housed in American collections, almost all of whose cultural affiliations have not been determined.[6] Museums abroad also contain many remains, both from Native North America and many other parts of the world, particularly former colonial territories. In France, for example, the Musée de l'Homme houses 18,000 skulls, including those of African chiefs and more than two hundred Native Americans from such groups as the Sioux and Navajo nations.[7] While various countries have adopted a range of policies relating to the preservation or repatriation of such remains, no country has developed a special forum to deal with claims for their return.

Two main possibilities present themselves when state-organized courts are used for adjudicating any dispute. One can employ courts that possess general jurisdiction, relying on their rules of procedure and the wide-ranging experience of their judges to address issues of every description. Such is the case, for example, with NAGPRA, which reposes jurisdiction for any disputes arising under the statute with the federal courts.[8] Alternatively, one can create forums that are unique to a particular class of disputes, ones in which the mandate, the evidentiary process, and the array of possible solutions are closely calibrated to the expertise and/or equitable concerns brought to the subject. Particularly when one is confronted with whole communities who may see the question at issue in deeply conflicting ways, the possibility of forming a tribunal that specializes in a given field may have much to commend it. Such is the case when we are confronted with disputes relating to the bodies of native peoples.

To suggest, as we shall here, that special courts would be appropriate to the matter of indigenous remains and DNA is, at least in the context of common law regimes, hardly a unique idea. Special courts have long existed, whether it was those employing merchants to decide disputes among fellow tradesmen in early British law, the religious courts whose rulings are not binding on state courts but whose solutions once accepted by both parties may be treated by state courts as enforceable contracts, or the hybridized out-of-court conciliation many divorce courts require of litigants. Currently there are traffic courts, drug courts, and family law courts specializing in those fields in many countries.

The rationale for courts with limited subject matter jurisdiction is often prompted by several concerns. How, after all, can one expect each judge—much less each juror—to be adept in the handling of every subject of litigation? How can creative remedies be fashioned when those with which a general court has experience are limited by tradition, statute, or the pressures of a bar confined by its own training and interests? If one is to propose that specialized courts are best suited to adjudicating the disposition of indigenous remains, it may be worthwhile first to consider the costs and benefits of such alternative forums; then to explore briefly several models that have been successfully employed in other domains; and finally to evaluate some concrete mechanisms that might best suit the issues, the parties, and the expert knowledge that come together when control over the remains of predecessors is to be assigned. Because the issue of adjudicating control over such remains is inseparable from broader issues of the relations between indigenous populations and the states within which they reside, it may also be worth considering what is due native peoples more broadly and how the establishment of specialized courts for this particular purpose may yield guidance for other mechanisms of reconciliation and fair dealing.

* * *

Courts tend to be generalists. A given court may receive a disproportionate number of cases on a particular topic and thus develop considerable experience in that field, as has the U.S. Court of Appeals for the Federal Circuit in Washington, DC, for example, in the field of administrative law, or the U.S. Court of Appeals for the Fourth Circuit in national security cases. Nevertheless, as courts of general jurisdiction, they tend (as in all common law countries) to rely on contending counsel to bring specialized knowledge to the trier of fact—although, more rarely, the court itself may appoint an expert or special master—or they may (as in most European systems) depend on the investigating magistrate to gather information in the dossier laid before a mixed panel of professional and lay jurors. Either way, two things tend to remain constant: the implementation of rules and remedies that are broadly composed for all types of cases—and that may or may not be fully appropriate to more specialized issues—and trust in the generalist rather than the specialist to make the ultimate decision. Much has been written about whether judges, and more particularly ordinary jurors, are capable of dealing with complex litigation (such as patent infringement, medical malpractice, or airline accidents) where highly skilled technicians may be called upon to testify, and much has been made of the seemingly odd notion that (as someone once said) jurors would not qualify as experts but are qualified to judge between the experts. Much, too, is made of the idea that a democracy may benefit from ordinary people being responsible for the determination of facts or (as in European-style systems) being seated alongside of—and capable of outvoting—trained judges in such determinations. And while studies have shown that jurors all too often do not comprehend the matters placed before them, there is no way of simply measuring the benefits of their participation for the larger democratic project.[9]

Running a cost-benefit analysis of specialized versus general jurisdiction forums cannot, therefore, be reduced to a simple formula or algorithm. What is possible, however, is to ask whether the rules of evidence applied in the latter are better set aside in favor of ones that may be developed by the former. For example, who will qualify as an expert may be too rigidly defined in general courts, whereas in an issue-specific forum those rules might be appropriately altered. Thus, a tribal elder who cannot speak as an expert on the age of human remains may nevertheless be allowed, in a more specialized forum, to testify as to those oral traditions that relate to their tribe's presence in the region and their customary ways of dealing with unidentified human remains. Indeed, oral history that may not be allowed in one forum may be regarded as helpful in another, or what qualifies as impermissible hearsay may be barred from consideration in one venue but regarded as useful information in another.

H. L. A. Hart, as we noted earlier, once said: "It is a feature of the human predicament that we labour under two connected handicaps whenever we seek to regulate, unambiguously and in advance, some sphere of conduct by means of general standards. . . . The first handicap is our relative ignorance of fact: the second is our relative indeterminacy of aim."[10] As to his first proposition, if one way to get at the most accurate facts is to open widely the bounds of relevance of a given case, then a more specialized forum may have certain advantages. For example, a general court of law whose rules of evidence will have arisen out of other contexts may preclude, as not germane to the issue of ownership, testimony on the felt sense of injury native people experience when seeing their ancestors' remains subjected to laboratory experiments. Or a general court may have developed (as American courts have in the case of many Native American disputes) the rule that access to a sacred site or exclusive control over a ritual or artifact must be proven to be a "necessary and indispensable" element of the native religion in order to receive acknowledgment.[11] A tribunal that has repeated experience with issues of native property, however, may fashion a much different standard for proving up one's interest or for assigning the burden of proof in these highly distinctive cases.

Hart's second notion—that of the indeterminacy of aim—may manifest itself differently in the two types of forums. If in general courts the aim is, for example, to decide who is at fault and then to apply standardized (even mandatory) penalties or awards, in a court of special issue the aim may instead be to place both parties back into a situation where they can best negotiate their differences. This is not to say that the general courts cannot or do not foster conciliation but rather that this is not commonly their primary aim. And since, if Hart is correct, accomplishing the law's goal is always elusive and not reducible to singular propositions, then a special court with more open-ended evidentiary and procedural rules may be in a better position to fashion novel remedies and encourage appropriate settlements.

It is here that the experience of a range of alternative forums may be enlightening, particularly since issues of native remains involve numerous countries within whose broader legal framework any special courts will have to fit. Although one could point to many other examples, there are three to which I will refer. (Admittedly, mine is a North American starting point, and I do not mean to suggest any superiority to these examples by focusing on them: they are offered as much to encourage others to supply examples of their own as to exemplify some of the advantages that may inhere in any forum running parallel to those of the state.) The three examples that will be discussed are the Indian Claims Commission, the Jewish Conciliation Board, and the dispute resolution forums of the Navajo and Hopi nations of the American Southwest.

* * *

In 1946, following recognition that earlier assimilationist policies had failed, the United States Congress tried a new stratagem. At that time, if an Indian tribe sought damages from the federal government for failing to honor its treaty commitments, the tribe had to get Congress to pass an act waiving the federal government's sovereign immunity, thereby allowing the government to be sued in a court of law. Under the sponsorship of Senator Roman Hruska of Nebraska, Congress acceded to the idea that if all Indian claims could be settled quickly the rationale for continued living on reservations—to preserve possible claims—would evaporate and the Indians would readily assimilate, their remaining lands being opened up to normal purchase and sale. A legal body called the Indian Claims Commission was, accordingly, created to hear cases. Its tenure was only supposed to last five years, and it could award only monetary damages, not land. As matters turned out, the press of cases was so great that the ICC's charter had to be extended multiple times.

By 1978, when the Commission was terminated and its pending docket of 170 cases assigned to the U.S. Court of Federal Claims, it had awarded $818,172,606.64 in judgments and had completed 546 dockets.[12]

By its title, the ICC would seem to have been less a formal court than some ill-defined adjudicative body. Although the ICC's procedural rules were not those of the federal or state courts and its personnel were not judges in the ordinary sense, Congress did set a number of conditions to its operation. Of particular relevance for our purposes are two provisions: The Commission could hear even "moral claims" against the U.S. government; and from any monetary award the Commission must deduct the value of items the federal government had given freely to the tribe, deductions that were called "gratuitous offsets." The first provision may seem to have been an act of contrition or accommodation by the government, whereas in fact its proponents argued that if Indians were allowed to sue *even* on moral claims they would be all the more eager to bring their actions against the United States to a timely conclusion and move off the reservations into mainstream American life. Similarly, the offsets were meant to underscore the seeming generosity of the government that extended beyond the formal requirements of treaties and subsequent agreements. So as the ICC set about its work it appeared to be limited by distinctive boundaries and guidelines. But since it also had certain elements of procedural flexibility, it was, in fact, able to extend itself in ways the originators failed to foresee, ways that may also suggest useful approaches to current issues of human remains.

The ICC took the moral claims provision rather seriously and proceeded to build a body of practice concerning its definition and scope. It did not hesitate to mark as immoral and thus compensable a wide variety of acts by the federal government over the course of many decades. As for the gratuitous offsets, it simply refused to apply them. Every five years, when Congress had to extend the ICC's mandate because of the huge backlog of cases, it told the Commission to apply the offsets, and every time the commissioners, obviously feeling them unfair, refused to do so, until near the end of the Commission's life when Congress finally capitulated on the issue. This history might, then, suggest two factors relevant to our concerns here, namely, that one can have a courtlike institution that nevertheless is not bound by the fact-finding procedures of the mainline courts, and that such a body may interpret its mandate in such a way as to shame those who would twist it to their own agenda or expand its mandate to fulfill its highest purpose. Thus it is possible to have a state-sponsored forum that is not hamstrung by the canons of the formal courts and one whose goal is to find solutions that are equitable rather than simply legal.

The second example is that of the Jewish Conciliation Board in New York City.[13] At the time of its establishment in 1920, many of the Jewish immigrants to New York were neither Orthodox practitioners of the faith comfortable taking their disputes to a religious law court (beth din), nor were they willing to endure the costs, delays, and unfamiliar formalities of the state courts. For them the Board was a welcome alternative: Its style was unceremonious, it was not bound by prior rulings, its costs were minimal, and its use of the same agreement employed in formal arbitration proceedings meant that its rulings would almost certainly be upheld should a losing party revive its case before a state court. Interestingly, the Board initially consisted of three conciliators: a lawyer (to ensure that decisions would indeed pass muster with the state courts if necessary), a rabbi (who gave the body a certain religious legitimacy without invoking formal Jewish law, or halacha), and a businessman (who, presumably, possessed the real-world approach of compromise, practicality, and common sense the professionals might lack). Later—in what one is tempted to consider a very American move—a psychiatrist was also seated on the board. Indeed, as the older immigrant population passed from the scene, the Board moved from the Lower East Side into the same building with Jewish Social Services in Midtown Manhattan and, for a time, found renewed life with the wave of Russian Jewish immigrants before closing down entirely in the 1980s.

In the many cases that have been reported from the court and in visits to it by several of my students over the years, it was clear that the Board focused on the individuals involved; attended both to their felt sense of injury *and* whether there were objective grounds for allowing an action; and was highly flexible in its proposed remedies. The presence of the rabbi and others may have helped shame some of the more contentious litigants into resolving their differences, and certainly the speed and cost-effectiveness of the proceedings were welcomed by all. But the important lesson for our purposes may not simply be one of flexibility of process and remedy; if the sort of people who serve as conciliators matches the concerns of the parties, the lesson is that informal social pressures may be more effective than formal legal rules in reaching a workable conclusion.

Critical issues are raised by courts like the Jewish Conciliation Board, in particular whether it is possible to be effective if the litigants do not share a common culture, religion, or set of interconnected social ties, and whether people from very different orientations and legal traditions will be willing to use a specialized forum unless it mimics the features of courts and mediators with which they have some familiarity. That is why our third example poses even more concerns as a model for human remains adjudication. For all the differences that may exist within their own tribes and among those who are more "traditional," "modern," or "in-between," indigenous forums like the Navajo Peacemaker Court and the Hopi Tribal Courts do serve communities that possess a common cultural base upon which they can build. That might seem to be far less the case if a scientist wants to run forensic experiments that a tribe resists or if a museum catering to an overwhelmingly white population wants to maintain a display of indigenous burial materials. But the dispute resolution mechanisms of indigenous peoples may nevertheless suggest certain forms of attending to disputes that a specialized forum may wish to consider.

In both the Navajo and Hopi tribunals a key question is how customary practice is to be addressed.[14] Both allow—even encourage—the use of custom while retaining a system of internal appellate review; and both have limited jurisdiction over non-tribesmen for various types of cases. But both employ an overall style of conciliation from which one might draw when confronted with creating special forums for issues of human remains and studies of contemporary DNA. For example, testimony about the fears native people have of the uses to which such research may be put is vital to working out cross-cultural problems. To many native peoples the fear is that, like the changing rules about blood quantum set by the federal government or their own tribe, individuals may be declared no longer members of the tribe if their DNA raises questions of sufficient biological attachment. Similarly, dating human remains may undercut a tribe's claim to have been on their land since "time immemorial," or at least before other claimants. It is true that DNA sampling, especially when carried out with the tribe's cooperation, may support their claim to governmental recognition.[15] But at the same time, fears as to the misuse of such findings have been exacerbated in the United States as a number of tribes have declared existing members no longer eligible for tribal membership in a bald attempt to limit the number of persons entitled to a share of casino or reservation resources.[16] Additionally, tribesmen may be concerned about the internal repercussions for the entire group of how their bodies and those of their ancestors are treated, repercussions that include questioning the powers and legitimacy of local religious personnel and the balance of powers within the group generally. If one were to draw from the experience of these courts and ones like them in many parts of the indigenous world, one might be able to imagine not only a mixed panel of specialist/mediators but also the development of rules of procedure that bring out the broader implications of a case than may be permitted in state courts.

For each of the three examples discussed one can find, in various parts of the world, numerous corollaries and alternatives. In West Africa, for example, the Kpelle use an adjudication model that allows litigants great scope in articulating their sense of injury and also offers an approach that appears effective because it proceeds very much like a therapeutic session.[17] In Japan, where conciliation was mandated during the Tokugawa regime and where going to court is still frowned upon, informal forums and the pressures of family and neighbors often resolve differences.[18] And in various parts of the Muslim world one finds alongside the Islamic law courts popularly attended sessions held even on the street by respected mediators.[19] Having special courts does not, as many of these examples suggest, mean courts run by specialists, helpful as their experience may be. What it does mean is that new, hybridized forums that will build a body of experience and be free to draw on multiple models that are not identical to those the formal courts of the jurisdiction employ may be best suited where substantial cultural differences are in play. Later we will see what some of those possibilities might look like, but there is one more broad-scale question that should be considered first.

* * *

The larger question is whether special courts—or existing state courts, for that matter—ought to be constructed so as to favor indigenous peoples in certain ways, whether by the distribution of burdens of proof or persuasion; by modifying the rules of evidence to give equal—or even favored—weight to the kind of testimony one side or the other may offer; or by opening the bounds of relevance so wide as to provide some sense of closure for past harm. If, to take just one example, human remains taken from a field of battle between federal and Indian forces nearly two hundred years ago have been kept in museum storage ever since, and a tribe has reconstituted itself only in order to get the right to build a casino on their land—using the return-of-burials issue as a vehicle for claiming their group identity and thus their right to recognition so the casino can be built—is there anything in this fact pattern that should lead one to give the Indians the benefit of the doubt in their litigation or to deny them any privileged consideration? In an attempt to address these issues, philosophers and political theorists from both the indigenous and nonindigenous communities have fashioned a number of arguments.

Native thinkers often take the position that ancient wrongs are still wrongs: that even if time may lead you to love thy neighbor you may still want him to return what his grandfather took from your grandfather. From this perspective time does not eradicate the underlying wrong, however much reconciliation may now be the common goal. Vine Deloria, Jr., and many other indigenous thinkers have, therefore, proposed a variety of approaches, many of which have found favor with their interlocutors.[20] For example, the museum at the University of British Columbia has an agreement with native peoples that they may bring food offerings to the spirits of those ancestors embraced in artifacts maintained in and by the museum and that they may do so in private. In other contexts it has been recognized that native rights extend beyond reservation lands when, for example, special periods are reserved for rituals to be held at off-reservation sacred sites from which nonnatives are precluded during those times. Others argue that indigenous groups are sovereign entities and that taking their materials is no different than the British appropriating the Elgin Marbles or the Belgians the sculptures of African tribal artists and that, at the very least, the standards developed nations have claimed for themselves ought to apply to native populations as well. From the viewpoint of the indigenous thinkers on these matters, the starting point is a vision of time and circumstance that gives priority to native customs and practices; should disagreement over something like the disposition of ancient remains be unresolved by the parties, then the balance should tip in the native peoples' favor given the historic injustices. Some of the most noteworthy political philosophers in the West take different approaches to the issues. The ideas of four such scholars—Joseph Raz, Michael Walzer, Jeremy Waldron, and John Rawls—are worth brief consideration.

Joseph Raz argues that any minority community, indigenous or otherwise, has no claim for special consideration in two respects. First, although the larger community owes minorities a duty of doing them no harm, the majority does not owe them a duty of preservation of their particular identity. To borrow a phrase, Raz appears not to want the state to play the role of "cultural game warden" simply because the minority is a distinctive entity. Second, at the same time, he says, individuals do have a right to the retention of their group's integrity and to preserve the opportunity to control their membership. In his own words:

> [M]ulticulturalism requires a political society to recognize the equal standing of all the stable and viable cultural communities existing in that society. This includes the need for multicultural political societies to reconceive themselves. There is no room for talk of a minority problem or of a majority tolerating the minorities. A political society, a state, consists—if it is multicultural—of diverse communities and belongs to none of them. While the relative size of the different communities affects the solutions to conflicts over resources and public spaces among them, none of them should be allowed to see the state as its own, or to think that the others enjoy their standing on sufferance.
>
> While incorporating policies of non-discrimination, liberal multiculturalism transcends the individualistic approach which they tend to incorporate, and recognizes the importance of unimpeded membership in a respected and flourishing cultural group for individual well-being.[21]

The implications of Raz's argument would seem to be one of noninterference in the viability of a membership group. However, if they are unable to preserve their own identity, then the state should do nothing for them that they have not been able to do for themselves. As for special forums considering cases of native remains, one would have to assume that Raz's position implies that the state should not use such vehicles to reinforce group identity: only the people themselves should be involved in maintaining their identity. By contrast, since the state should not actively interfere with group membership, Raz would appear to have no objection to an indigenous group bringing suit on behalf of its members for any number of alleged wrongs, provided that the process is not a leg-up to the state reinforcing the group's existence. Precisely what that would translate into in a court of special jurisdiction is not addressed. Similarly, how one determines which indirect acts either support or undermine group identity is left unstated.

Michael Walzer appears close to Raz when he states that "majorities have no obligation to guarantee the survival of minority cultures. . . . [There] is no reason to come to their rescue; they have a claim, indeed, to physical but not to cultural security." Every individual and every group, he argues, should emphasize more than one feature of their identity, and he concludes by stating that "our common humanity will never make us members of a single universal tribe. The crucial commonality of the human race is particularism."[22] Walzer's emphasis on individualism does not necessarily preclude associations—whether cultural, political, or religious—from attending to their own concerns, but it does suggest that any special consideration for native rights needs to be seen against the backdrop of personal freedom, not collective entitlements. For purposes of our topic, the position of Walzer, like that of Raz, does not neatly translate into clear approaches to the return of native remains or the role of science in the investigation of native DNA. But it could be used to support the proposition that, once again, it is only the individual who constitutes the basis of society and therefore no special protections need be accorded the concerns of entities such as tribal groups beyond those to which any other association would be entitled.

Jeremy Waldron signals much the same approach, arguing that the state should not, by reifying the culture of a group, freeze it in place as if it were a pure entity immune to change from within and without.

> To put it crudely, we need culture, but we do not need cultural integrity. . . . In general, there is something artificial about a commitment to *preserve* minority cultures. Cultures live and grow, change and sometimes

wither away; they amalgamate with other cultures, or they adapt themselves to geographical or demographic necessity. To *preserve* a culture is often to take a favored "snapshot" version of it, and insist that this version must persist at all cost, in its defined purity, irrespective of the surrounding social, economic, and political circumstances.[23]

Waldron's position would presumably apply to the majority culture as well as that of minorities. Would he eliminate the concept—to which both conservative and liberal justices in the United States often refer—that "the traditions of our people" ought to play a role in certain legal decisions? Is recognition of a right really a freezing in place? What if that which is preserved is one of a group's mechanisms for dealing with change? In the case of native peoples, identifying the culture in question is usually straightforward, and any assumption that they are unchanging and simply subject to a dominant polity's ability to render them static only perpetuates a misleading stereotype. Still, if the only protections, say, against intrusion into the group's concerns over their ancestors and their own identity are those arising out of the conqueror's culture, it is not because of preservation for its own sake that allowances for difference ought to find legal support in an appropriate forum.

If each of the preceding authors seems to propound if not a masked assimilationism at least a reluctance to disrupt the universalism and cosmopolitanism of their views, John Rawls, by comparison, argues that some assistance is due the protection of peoples' cultures provided their societies are "liberal" and "decent" and not "outlaw states," "burdened societies," or "benevolent absolutisms." Unlike the emphasis on individuals in *A Theory of Justice*, in his later book *The Law of Peoples* the focus is clearly on collectivities. But Rawls is vague as to which groups qualify, why in the international or indigenous context the individual—so favored in the domestic context—is now submerged in the collective, and what the "duty of assistance" would mean when the questions are ones of identity and cultural maintenance.[24] One cannot, for example, easily move from his general concept to answers about the rights of science versus indigenous control of human remains and DNA.

Each of the above scholars seems to assume that if only we apply neutral principles to all groups the need to accord special protections for the culture of any particular group should disappear. But two quite obvious problems persist: (1) that past actions have put many groups—particularly indigenous peoples—at so great a disadvantage in the preservation of their identity as to render subsequent "neutrality" altogether insufficient to the task of creating true equality; and (2) that special consideration is not incompatible with other legal doctrines that recognize, say, the unique nature of land in upholding a contract for sale of real estate or that custody of a child may take into consideration the cultural or religious heritage that only similarly situated guardians may fully prepare the child to join. To the first point, various judges have noted (in equal pay claims, for example) that to treat entities identically when they start from an unequal base is only to perpetuate the inequality. Native peoples who have had their lands stolen and who may at best receive only the same market value as in any other taking are not being treated equally: Their unequal position is simply being continued. And as to the second point, failure to make truly available the same mechanisms for perpetuating identity to native peoples is nothing more than slow-motion strangulation of the sources needed if actual equality is to be achieved.

While one may disagree as to the extent that the preservation of indigenous cultures justifies special consideration, it may, at the same time, be unfair to ask of philosophers—indigenous or Western—to come up with a grand theory of sovereignty, rights, and the relation of science to culture from which one could easily read out solutions to every point of contention. The first question, therefore, may not be how such matters should be decided but who should decide them and by what procedural and evidentiary means. Obviously the choice of forum and its methods may determine the outcomes, which may be all the more reason to attempt a relatively clean slate as one enters the field. That is, one could implement a new forum for a new set of issues with a new set of remedies and a new set of deciding personnel, drawing perhaps on the sort of examples we have discussed. To do so is, again, hardly unique in Western legal systems. The history of the British common law is one of new prerogative courts being generated that could offer causes of action and remedies existing courts could not—and developing new rules of procedure and specializations along the way. Similar courts have been formed in other legal traditions as well. The questions to be addressed, therefore, are: What modes of fact-determination might be most appropriate to a special tribunal? And if the case can be made for distinctive modes of proceeding, can we really say that by and large the creation of such new forums would indeed be the best way to adjudicate issues related to human remains?

* * *

New panels could have new procedures. Experts, for example, could utilize an extension of Australia's so-called hot-tub approach, in which the experts meet, sort out which issues are truly in contention, and assure the forum that all germane viewpoints are indeed presented, not just those of contending counsel, an investigating magistrate, or a single expert chosen by the court. The forum itself should have both native and nonnative members; be ready to adjourn for informal conversations; develop its own rituals of conciliation; and look beyond the singular issue before them to see if there are more systemic problems underlying the dispute that could either be addressed by the forum or be sent along to other venues. Suggested remedies should be creative, even experimental: Can new burial places acceptable to the native peoples be found for the remains? Can limits be set for the distribution of DNA findings? Have all parties inquired as to how others have resolved this problem? Can both native peoples and researchers apply for certain grants jointly and thereby establish long-term contractual goals? Can an appropriate ritual of reconciliation be built into the resolution of the dispute? Often what is sought by native peoples is not simply restitution or clarification of ownership but an apology, and such a forum may be better positioned than state courts to conduce such expressions of regret.[25] Indeed, could such forums, though initially set up to consider only these issues, not establish a pattern for a broader range of cross-cultural disputes? Through more specialized forums, the theories of what is owed native peoples in this regard would be tested in real-world situations and may have as dramatic an effect on those theories as has been the case when social scientists and other experts have become involved in similar forums.[26]

It would be naïve, of course, to imagine that such forums will be without their potential downside. We know from other examples that experts or arbitrators may have too much influence or compete for lucrative assignments and—as has been the experience in international commercial arbitration—thereby undermine the whole thrust of the project.[27] Not all issues will be susceptible to consensual resolution: If the forum does not require parties to agree to their decision, further litigation in state courts will go forward; and if the parties must agree to be bound by the decision, they may avoid the forum altogether. Special courts are not the same as alternative dispute resolution forums, even though they may partake of some of the advantages and disadvantages of those mechanisms.[28] They should, however, be free to establish law (which mediation cannot), but they should not be easily dominated by the powerful. Creating an environment of trust in the forum's fairness may be its most important challenge.

It is in this spirit that one might begin to think about some of the features a special forum might adopt when confronted with cases involving the remains of indigenous peoples. Among these are:

1. The presumption should be that human remains that can, to a reasonable degree of certainty, be identified with existing native groups should be at the disposition of such groups. The native groups need not be ones recognized under other provisions of state or national law, but they must have some internally acknowledged leadership who can bring the claim on behalf of all. Ancient remains that cannot be connected to any existing group ought not to trigger a presumption in favor of either party, but historic remains whose provenance its holder cannot establish should be presumed subject to repatriation.[29]

2. The standard for admitting evidence should be one that allows all usefully informative written or oral testimony. The forum may develop boundaries of admissibility over the course of time but should maintain a very open-ended concept of evidence, erring on the side of too much information from a variety of sources rather than too little.

3. The level of proof required should be neither a preponderance of the evidence (as in common law civil cases) nor a virtual certainty (as in Continental courts). However, in the interests of equity and historic justice—and in full recognition that their resources are almost always unequal to those of their opponents—nonnative litigants should have to meet a higher level of persuasion than that

required of the native claimants whose ancestors' interests they represent.[30]

4. The forum should bear in mind that, as in the experience of many small-claims courts, it is often the opportunity to be heard (to "have one's day in court") that is vital to native litigants. Toward that end the tribunal should hear as wide a range of testimony as is feasible.

5. The tribunals should be creative in their physical arrangements. That is, they should consider seating around a table rather than in hierarchical positions and should employ any other format that facilitates mutual understanding among the parties.

6. Expertise should be very widely defined, with ordinary native witnesses accorded no less participation than credentialed individuals.

7. Every effort should be made to fashion a result that addresses the concerns of all parties, the history of past decisions for a range of native apprehensions being no less important than the interests of curators, scientists, or commercial enterprises.

8. The tribunal should retain continuing jurisdiction over any dispute, revisiting it if one or both parties have grounds for seeking additional guidance. Informal consultation for oversight of the resolution may also be channeled through others authorized by the court to assist the parties.

Many issues will remain to be resolved: What if any appellate structure should be available to review the special courts' decisions? If local tribunals rule in markedly different ways, what if any system of regularizing approaches will be necessary or desirable so potential researchers, native litigants, and entrepreneurs can reasonably predict the implications of their actions? If there is both native and nonnative representation on the panel, how shall each be chosen and their votes allocated?[31]

Each nation's forum will have to develop its own approaches; each will have to consider its own systemic impact. The Indian Claims Commission had a dramatic effect on anthropological theory as experts had to rethink what it meant under the statute to be a "tribe, band, or other organized entity." The Jewish Conciliation Board had to rethink what it meant to feel wronged. And the native courts of the American Southwest have had to rethink whether custom is stultifying or liberating, flexible or constricting, beneficial to the few or attentive to the most vulnerable. Any forum that tries to address native/nonnative disputes will face similar, if not more trying, issues. Hopefully, they may contribute significantly to the development of more realistic theories of native rights generally. Carving out a forum that starts afresh, whose mandate is fairness and not just adjudication of rights, and whose decision makers represent a proper range of likely constituencies may set a pattern not only for these special disputes but also for a style of reconciliation that will honor the best of all parties' ancestors. Frequently under attack through the choice of a forum not of their own making, native peoples find the preservation of their communities seriously undermined. Just as control over their membership and custody of their children, or jurisdiction over taxation and environmental rules, are essential to maintaining their cultural integrity, so, too, in one of those most intimate of collective engagements—control of their loved ones' bodies—any untoward assault can be especially hurtful. If the term "community" is to mean anything in the American imaginary, respect for this aspect is worthy of the most serious attention.

6

Valuing Native Culture

A Legislative Proposal

What is it worth? The very question seeks to equate one substance or activity with another, thereby enabling exchange but potentially jeopardizing relationships. For if what an object or act conveys is identity, relationship, status, or legitimate authority, the very translation may put each of those features at risk. How, then, is one to segregate the meaning of such material and physical elements from their "pure" exchange value? How is one to preserve the relationships and vision of an orderly world they may entail from their commercialization? And how, if one is prepared to recognize that money is not a universal medium of exchange but a highly specific and limited one, are we to distinguish those situations where it is relevant from those in which it ought not to play a role? Particularly when we are dealing with artifacts that are central to a community's identity, it is imperative to think about the collective interest and to apply criteria of judgment accordingly. By focusing on the intellectual production of native peoples, we can see these issues at work and consider how, by bringing culture more fully into the discussion, one might be able to formulate laws that address the role of shared objects in the concept of community.

* * *

In my first year of law school, Professor Richard A. Posner (later a federal appellate judge) picked me out of a hundred and fifty students to ask, "Mr. Rosen, what is your life worth?" I knew what I was supposed to say: that we could compute my future earnings based on education and professional accomplishment, assess my current living standard and project compensation for survivors accordingly, and that actuarial tables and medical statistics were but the marketplace's invisible hand revealed. To Posner's query about the value of my life, however, I responded: "In what cause?" When the giggling died down

Posner indicated that surely one could use the available economic data to compute a perfectly workable price. I replied that I might give my life freely for someone close to me or for a cause I held dear, while in other situations even a very large sum of money would seem inadequate. When Posner persisted in trying to elicit a basis for actual numbers, I found myself recalling a passage from my favorite legal text, Lewis Carroll's *Alice in Wonderland*: "'Write that down,' the King said to the jury, and the jury eagerly wrote down all three dates on their slates, and then added them up, and reduced the answer to shillings and pence."[1] Clearly, I thought, Posner's economic approach was trying to measure incommensurables, to reduce one kind of thing to another through the universal solvent of money, and that his was but another example of the great American need to quantify, if not monetize, everything.

In one sense the monetary valuation of a life is absurd, while in another it is perfectly understandable. It is absurd because the basis of valuation, when portrayed as immanent, is in fact deeply cultural: no universal theory of economics or logic can be relied upon to alchemically convert injury into dollars or pounds or euros.[2] In some instances the most appropriate compensation may be a heartfelt recognition of the wrong, in others a demonstration that the conduct leading to the death will not be repeated. If, as Posner's approach implies, evaluation is basically left to the experts, it may, of course, have the advantage of being subject to rational discussion—provided always that you accept the experts' premises. Such valuation is also comprehensible if it does not have to mean that money takes the place of life, only that it addresses some of the consequences of the loss of life. (That is why, under those circumstances, perhaps the proper question for Posner to have asked would have been: "Given that it has already happened, what is your *death* worth—to others?") Indeed, if there is a moral to my encounter with Posner's inquiry as to the value of my life, it may be that an answer purporting to be a matter of total neutrality and rational calculation is, in fact, at once arbitrary, societally entangled, and (notwithstanding claims to utter objectivity) revelatory of the cultural assumptions on which any valuation depends. This is especially true where a history of vexed dealings colors both ownership and evaluation. And nowhere is this truer than in assessing the value of items produced by native peoples whose well-being is bound up in repatriating those material vehicles of their identity that currently lie in the hands of outsiders.

Monetization does not mean that we cannot have multiple ways of thinking about a subject even when we measure only one aspect of it against some economic indicator. To take a somewhat extreme example: for societies in which blood money takes the place of punishment, it may be the avoidance of continual feuding, the amelioration or sub-stitution of intense emotions, or a direct challenge to the ideals of for-giveness that take precedence over monetary compensation.[3] In such societies, people may prefer to limit centralized power by leaving the choice of punishment or reparation, hedged round by local custom, in private hands.[4] Indeed, differences of valuation, broadly conceived, can mark the fault line between cultures. For example, in 1883, when the United States Supreme Court ruled that an Indian tribe, in the exercise of its inherent sovereignty, was free to punish a killer by requiring him to support the deceased's family, Congress took away from the tribes the power of deciding such matters, believing that compensation for murder was barbarous and that the civilized thing to do was to hang the offender by the neck until he is dead.[5]

In many societies—especially small-scale tribal groups—objects are vital not as commodities but rather for the relationships of exchange and prestige they symbolize, and removal of the objects from local interplay is injurious to personal identity, social solidarity, and a felt sense of order.[6] So long as we do not imagine that translation into dollars is necessitated by nature or the capacity of market forces to reach the uniquely correct result and that any compensatory scheme is deeply connected to the his-tory and sociocultural system in which it is embedded, conversion of harm to money is not to be scorned out of hand. But when we do go about evaluating and equilibrating incommensurables, whether in civil or in criminal matters, the questions that necessarily arise include: What common denominator can be used? What cultural assumptions are in-corporated in our belief that the exchange of money or punishment is the most appropriate response to harm? If money is not the only gauge for valuation, other remedies are available, including apology, forgive-ness, rehabilitation, altered safety and marketing practices, or rituals of purification and re-inclusion. Each takes on a distinctive cultural and emotional tone as the meaning of each remedy takes on local coloration.[7]

Compensation may thus take various forms. For example, some non-Western legal systems make use of a right of preemption. Thus in some Muslim countries, when a property comes up for sale the right to purchase it may be accorded one or more neighbors because they may need to serve as protectors against communal violence, helpmates in daily life, a likely source of spouses for one's dependents, and witnesses or intermediaries in a legal dispute. The price may have to match that paid by any third party, and litigation may be needed to force the owner to turn over the property to the preemptor, but the importance of neighbors in such a system still takes precedence over subsidiary concerns.[8] In other cultures, a portion of the monetary penalty for a marital dispute may be imposed even on the spouse found not responsible in the belief that domestic tranquility will be more likely if the offending party does not have reason to take the loss out on the partner. So, too, what constitutes harm, particularly as balanced against another's freedom of expression, is variable: troubling questions of freedom versus compensation arise when music rehearsals are too loud for a neighbor or when a local public utility impinges on the use of an adjacent property.[9] Similarly, an object of collective value may be within the control of its owner but barred from sale outside the group identified with it. And, of course, a property may be taken for a public purpose by the government in a forced sale, the fair market value paid at that time being different from what the owner may have hoped to gain in the future.

If even money can, therefore, stand for a relationship, a valued avenue to peace, or a symbol of collective identity or personal self-worth, the way in which a society fashions its translation from "object of engagement" to "object of exchange" thus teases up a whole series of interconnected social and cultural expectations. The specific version of this issue that will concern us here is whether the intellectual productions of indigenous peoples are an exception to the general principles of ownership and valuation commonly used in nonnative legal settings and, if so, what legislative approaches may be most appropriate when such groups are involved.[10] Moreover, in the fraught history of native-colonial encounters, any scheme must balance the morally commended with the practical if the goal is to ameliorate rather than exacerbate past errors. Before considering possible legislation with such an aim, it may, however, be helpful to look at a few examples of the special circumstances that may apply to cases involving native peoples.

Indigenous groups frequently seek access to a sacred site located outside tribal lands, the conjuncture of ritual and space being indissoluble in their cultures. Elsewhere, tribal interest in an object of traditional design or exclusive control of a regional plant has occasioned suits for the protection of the collectivity's interests.[11] But monetary compensation or even land swaps are often deemed inappropriate by the natives. In what is perhaps the most noteworthy instance, the award of millions of dollars to the Sioux for their sacred Black Hills has never been touched by the tribe because the land itself is regarded as inalienable.[12] In still other cases artifacts sold at auction by nonnative possessors reach prices that native peoples cannot reasonably match.

Whether it is opposition to pipelines running under tribal lands or lax pollution standards affecting tribal enterprises, ecological concerns, too, displace mere compensation as an acceptable resolution. Efforts by nonnative governments to restrict the practice of traditional medicine, resource extraction, or customary law are similarly regarded as incommensurable with monetary rewards. And from the natives' point of view, the history of depredations by whites and their governments constitutes the indispensable backdrop to any scheme affecting tribal interests. In this regard formulating an approach to the cultural property rights of indigenous peoples necessarily teases up a number of concerns no legislative or judicial proposal can afford to ignore.[13]

The situation of native peoples is, therefore, indeed a special case, one that affects legislative and judicial approaches to their intellectual and cultural property interests.[14] Not only were hundreds of treaties signed with Native American groups; the U.S. Supreme Court from early in the nineteenth century recognized the tribes as sovereign entities notwithstanding the relinquishment or divestment of some of their powers. Treaties were, however, repeatedly violated by white America, and compensation schemes have rarely succeeded. More than five hundred tribes are federally recognized in the United States, and others are in the process of applying for inclusion, many of whom have long had contentious claims against the federal government.

Realism, particularly in the American context, thus commends recognition that, to a considerable extent, money is the solvent through which exchange takes place, and it is therefore naïve to expect that objects of indigenous origin can simply be pried loose from owners without any compensation. Even if "all property is theft," a workable solution to the return of native objects will require some exchange. To fairly engage material as well as cultural concerns—and to align them with existing schemas of rights and obligations—requires a balancing act, though not one of simply reducing all of the variables to shillings and pence. A legislative program that achieves such a balance may at the very least be more of a guide than a solution and at most a framework within which both parties and adjudicators can weigh that which can be monetized with that which is regarded as inalienable. Moreover, legislators, unlike judges, may base their laws on cultural precepts and historic wrongs, matters that are especially appropriate where native people are involved. The following, therefore, is a proposed statute intended to speak to these concerns.

THE INDIGENOUS CULTURAL PROPERTY ACT

DEFINITIONS

Indigenous groups (hereafter also *the group* or *groups*): Any band, tribe, or otherwise organized native entity that has received governmental recognition or can demonstrate that there has at any time been government-to-government interaction with said group.

Object of indigenous origin (hereafter also *the object*): Any material object or distinctive design, not including land, for which an indigenous group can establish a prima facie case for origination.

Right of preemption: The right to intervene in the sale of any object of indigenous origin and to purchase said object as set forth in the statute.

Droit de suite: The right to a portion of the proceeds when an object of indigenous origin is sold to successive purchasers.

STATUTORY PROVISIONS

1. Indigenous groups shall have a right of first refusal to the purchase of any object of indigenous origin that is offered for sale, whether the object comes to market through public or private offering.

   (a) A group may give public notice of its interest in invoking the right of preemptive purchase should a particular object of indigenous origin come up for sale, in which case the sale shall be postponed for sixty days in order to give the group time to raise the necessary funds to exercise its preemptive right.

(b) The group may assign its right of preemption for a particular purchase to a public or nonprofit institution, such as a museum or university.

(c) Notice must be published for sales of an object of indigenous origin by public or nonprofit institutions. Public notice is also required for private sales, whether direct or through an intermediary, if the sale involves an object a group has given notice that it may wish to obtain by right of pre-emption. Sale of any object that fails to accord with this provision shall be subject to nullification.

(d) No object obtained by right of first refusal may subsequently be sold or otherwise alienated by the group without authority from its governing body.

(e) The price of an object to be obtained through the right of preemption shall be the lowest price that is (1) publicly set by the seller, (2) the highest price offered by private or public sale, or (3) the average price both parties agree to be set by a panel of three individuals, one chosen by the seller, one by the indigenous group, and one chosen by the other panel members.

2. The Federal government shall establish a fund for the benefit of any indigenous group to assist in their purchase of objects of indigenous origin.

3. Any object created by an identified artist who is recognized by his or her indigenous group as a member and for which that group has given public notice of its interest to purchase such objects as may come on the market shall, upon resale, be subject to a *droit de suite* calculated as a percentage of the sale price to be established by agreement or legislation, such sale price being shared equally by the group and the individual artist. Upon his or her death the artist's share shall be accorded to the group. Any resale that does not afford the opportunity for a *droit de suite* shall be null and void.

Several comments on these provisions are in order.

Definitions always raise the difficulty of either being too specific or too general.[15] In an attempt to err on the side of greater inclusiveness, the characterization of eligible groups and their relationships to over-arching governments is kept intentionally wide, owing in part to the depredations of states in the past and the value of native stewardship in the present. Instead of focusing on direct compensation for harm done to native peoples, the proposed statute concentrates on making objects of indigenous importance available to the originating groups in an atmosphere of mutual consideration. The statute focuses on objects rather than abstract intellectual property. However, if an idea, process, or version of a design—such as a harvestable plant extract—exists in a distinctive form associated with the creative input of an indigenous group, the statute is intended to include such embodiments.

The concept of a right of preemption for fair market value underscores both the priority accorded native groups to restoration of their cultural objects and fair market valuation notwithstanding the history of present ownership. Real property (land, buildings, etc.) is not included in this statute.[16] The law would thus cover public as well as private sellers, since many objects are in the hands of individual collectors and, whether they are of dubious or legitimate provenance, are of vital concern to the identity and well-being of the indigenous group. The provision covers any resale, including that of an object initially received as a gift. The provisions for notice, which may be worked out in the regulations relating to the statute, may necessitate formation of a vehicle similar to the National Stolen Art File or the Art Loss Register, so both holders and sellers, who will be expected to exercise due diligence, are aware of the implications of any offer for sale in which they may engage.

Many groups may be unable to purchase or curate objects and are willing to have museums or other nonprofit institutions act as guardians for the objects, hence the capacity to assign their right of preemption to such institutions. Because many objects were lost to indigenous groups by government action or inaction, some responsibility for their initial loss must be borne by that government, hence the appropriateness of their assistance in funding the repatriation of such objects. If representatives are chosen to set the price of the object, they may be drawn from any background, though experts in the valuation of such objects should be favored.

Finally, in alignment with developing international standards, a form of *droit de suite* will help to allay potential conflict between an artist and the artist's own group, both of whom have had an interest in the production of a given object, believing, with Virginia Woolf, that "[m]asterpieces are not single solitary births; they are the outcome of many years of thinking in common, of thinking by the body of the people, so the experience of the mass is behind the single voice."[17]

The statute does leave certain vexing issues unaddressed. For example, not all of the members of a given indigenous community may see matters identically. Disputes over who controls the objects, who speaks for the group, and who should receive what share of any compensation are regrettably, if inevitably, no less frequent among native peoples than any others. Mediation and arbitration may be the preferred methods for addressing these disputes, but the courts may be called upon to decide issues of representation as in many similar intellectual property matters.[18]

There are several reasons for addressing these issues through federal legislation rather than leaving matters to existing statutes or case law. If one accepts the premise that valuation is possible, one may be forced to accept the conclusion that even life is convertible to dollars and cents. In such instances the courtroom is an appropriate venue for settling such matters. But for so special a case as indigenous peoples, who have been subjected to colonial depredations and whose place in the body politic and imaginary of the dominant population remains ambiguous at best and racist at worst, it may very well be that settling ownership rights and valuations are best left to legislatures rather than courts. Legislatures are not only permitted to speak to the moral sentiments of a nation; their actions may properly be based on a degree of arbitrary choice, as opposed to courts, which, in such policy-heavy circumstances, cannot appear to be independently concerned by issues of morality and historic injustice. This is not at all to suggest that legislatures are either wise or fair in their treatment of native peoples. But at least if matters are approached legislatively, then one may be able, for example, to offer native peoples a preemptive right to buy in artifacts that originated with them—perhaps even with some government support (effectively resulting in a discount from fair market value and an indirect form of reparation).

One can rationalize such statutory assistance in a variety of ways: as a moral requirement that we care for each other's patrimony, as compensation for past harm, or as a practical measure for ensuring native stewardship. Indeed, it is on such grounds that other legislative programs have been designed (as, for example, those that favor the hiring of native peoples or offer protections for the marketing of their artistic productions).[19] Whatever the chosen method, the distinctiveness of the native situation probably should take precedence over simply hoping to preserve the Indians' valid concerns by melding them into the laws governing all other populations.

The proposed statute recognizes that unless some payments change hands—some valuation is made of the invaluable—no restoration of native objects may take place. Realism demands that some compromise be made. But if the history of the world's indigenous peoples suggests anything, it is that there are indeed values—and thus valuations—that resist simple monetary equivalence, and a significant degree of deference to indigenous forms of evaluation and current ownership of indigenous heritage must be forthcoming so that progress may be made in constructing an environment of mutual trust. Legislation, such as that proposed here, would constitute both a practical step in that direction and a timely acknowledgment that cultural factors—including the protection of those material objects vital to a people's sense of community—have a place in the law alongside historical and moral considerations.

7

The Shortage Is Not Only of Water

Three stories:

Story No. 1: Early in my initial fieldwork in Morocco I undertook a study of the local irrigation system, something material I could observe and measure while still learning my way around the language and culture. With help from the local court expert on property, who was also one of my language teachers, I was able to accompany the *jarri*, the man who oversaw the local irrigation system, as he made his daily rounds. The *jarri* explained the timing and distribution of the system to me very clearly. Yet when we arrived at one man's plot he turned off the water. When I suggested that the man's allotment was not yet completed the *jarri* simply replied that the owner had enough water for now.

Story No. 2: The men gathered outside the mayor's office were clearly involved in some sort of dispute. When I approached one of them I was told that they all owned land below the small Moroccan city but disagreed as to when the water held back from the municipal swimming pool should be released each day such that it would arrive during the period when one or the other group would be entitled to all of the water then available. While waiting to see the local official, both sides joked with one another and in no way, then or later, betrayed any significant animosity.

Story No. 3: Following my second year of law school, while serving as a summer intern to an American Indian litigation group, I was asked by the lead attorney in a case challenging the distribution in the entire Colorado River system to research the regime governing the allocation of the river's waters. I immediately responded by saying that undoubtedly those who perfected their claims first had priority rights, that they could move water separately from the land, but that they had to make beneficial use of their entitlement. When he asked how I could know that I said because that is how it works in Morocco. At the time I thought I was joking. It turned out I was not.

* * *

The water distribution system of the American West came from Morocco. It came via Spain, Mexico, and the goldfields of California. Although various aspects were lost along the way and others were altered by local circumstances, similarities remain, both in the basic rules and the problems the formal system left unaddressed. In this chapter I want to consider how these two systems, stemming as they do from a common base, have addressed what might seem to be lacunae in the rules of water distribution and, in doing so, to explore in what ways this system fits with other aspects of the societies and legal regimes of these two widely separated cultures. By comparing several of their features— including the implications for dispute settlement and responses to ecological change—we may also be able to cast some light on the over- all picture we have of each of these societies and their respective sense of community. While solutions to the problems each continues to face are not readily available from their common origins, comparison may nevertheless suggest the areas, beyond technology and existing legal regimes, where alterations in their structure should be considered.

The linkage between water regimes in Morocco and the American West is, of course, historical, not inevitable: it is not that similar ecolo- gies require similar irrigation systems, or that the systems are utterly separable from the broader cultures within which they are entwined. It is true that there are distinct similarities between the arid zones of North Africa and the American West. In North Africa, where rainfall varies enormously from one month or year to the next, localized droughts are not uncommon, and an old saying holds that even a king cannot survive three successive years of drought. In the western United States, the cur- rent drought is described as the worst in 1,200 years, with sources like the Colorado River being at their lowest ebb in ages.[1] Improved reduc- tion in evaporation levels, increased digging of wells to tap groundwater, and minor alterations in the crops raised in such places as California's Central Valley are clearly insufficient to meet the current crisis. Under- standing the social and cultural context within which both the Moroc- can system and its American variant developed may prove necessary to any genuine resolution.

The historical connection between the irrigation systems of Morocco and the western United States is clear. When the Moors invaded Spain they took the North African water scheme with them. From there it went to Mexico and then to the goldfields of California, where, according to the customary practice of the miners, it became the basis for water law throughout most of the American West.[2] The foundational scheme that both initially shared centers on three main principles: People who established their claims first and make beneficial use of their water take priority over later claimants; water can be moved separately from the land; and prior appropriators get their full allotment before later ones get any. In short, no "shared poverty"—a harsh if realistic doctrine. However, like any legal design, not every situation that might arise can be covered by a rule, not every rule (however logical) is isolated from the relationships it entails, and not every relationship is wanting in a series of cultural assumptions that span multiple domains. Among the common factors that have been worked out differently in Morocco and the American West, several are particularly worthy of consideration: (1) the role of cross-cutting affiliations that ameliorate the harsher aspects of water rights; (2) the relation between private ownership of water rights and the need for cooperation even with one's competitors; and (3) the place that water occupies in the culture's vision of the larger social and natural world. For all their shared origins and environmental similarities, the differences between Morocco and America cannot be ignored, especially the concept of property and the differential roles of science, technology, and sociolegal relations in each of the cultures involved.

Moroccan water law focuses on the individual owner of a given allotment. There is no superordinate governance of the system, each localized portion having distinct procedures and personnel.[3] Usage must be personally effected and maintained: as the Arabic saying goes, "if a man is away his right is away." Such an emphasis constitutes a reflection of a culture in which each parcel of land is named, each individual's web of associates defines him, and each potential intrusion into a person's domain requires constant vigilance. Structurally flexible and deeply embedded in a never-ending quest for a network of mutual obligations, "the Moroccan passion for organizing everything in terms of the head-on encounter of individuals within a general, universalistic moral-legal code, which is used as a basis for forming contracts, arguing issues, deciding conflicts, maximizing options, and adjusting opportunistically to passing reality, runs through every aspect of local life." In what Clifford Geertz goes on to call an "environment of agonistic individualism," "Moroccan [social] integration comes down to mediating relations among a field of competing individuals, each with a somewhat different basis of power and each scrambling to make his way within the general rules of the game by his own wit and resources."[4]

This form of Moroccan individualism, though sharing a number of features with that of American culture, differs from the latter in certain key features that affected its integration into the water law of the western states. Indeed, when Moroccan water law made its way to the American West, it encountered a distinctly American version of "possessive individualism": for all the romance of "community"—frontier cooperation, collective barn-building, militia-based defense—the Tocquevillian image of encapsulating families and individualized ownership played into a water regime in which cross-cutting social ties were made largely irrelevant.[5] Tocqueville himself put it this way: "Individualism is a reflective and peaceable sentiment that disposes each citizen to isolate himself from the mass of those like him and to withdraw to one side with his family and his friends, so that after having thus created a little society of his own, he willingly abandons society at large to itself."[6] To this, Americans added the ostensible solution to any shortage of resources: technology.

Belief in science and engineering sits well with the ways in which Americans imagine their identity to be inscribed on and validated by the land they occupy. If a landscape painting can portray not so much the features of a physical terrain as the naturalized imprint of human enclosure and cultivation, so, too, the construction of dams and canals can seem but the help rendered unto Mother Nature by her human overseers. Europeans and Americans often credit themselves with scientific and technological innovation. But many of the methods and devices that have had such an impact on the American West's development originated in the Arab world, the creation of a water regime being far from the only such contribution. In mathematics, medicine, astronomy, and optics, the Arabs' advances in the eighth to thirteenth centuries were far ahead of those in the Christian Western world. But there is also a crucial difference in the purposes to which such knowledge has long been directed and the ways in which that focus is integrated with other aspects of the overall culture. For while such advances may, by the time of the scientific revolution, have been stimulated to a substantial degree in the West by the pursuit of knowledge about physical forces that are separable from their social consequences, in the Arabo-Berber world the focus has long remained on the human relationships such knowledge facilitates. Thus experimentation not directed to social ends was secondary to ideas and devices that hold a community together.[7]

Both systems, of course, have had to cope with limited supplies of water. In the American context the solution to insufficient water or maldistribution is thus embraced in engineering and the laws of water ownership: interconnected social bonds largely fall out of the equation, to be replaced by centralized institutions and impersonal rules. From the Moroccan perspective, however, exclusive reliance on technology and property law appears insufficient, to say nothing of unwise. Accordingly, water law was not only about resource technology. Seen only from the rules of beneficial use and distribution, the focus may appear highly individuated; by privileging those who come first, personal property rights may appear conclusive. But the Moroccans knew that the legal benefits afforded early beneficial users must be balanced with ties of kinship and alliance, prudent discretion, and flexible rules to ensure that today's latecomers will be tomorrow's helpmates. Just as America's Founders knew that without virtuous citizens no governmental structure alone could forestall the abuse of power, so, too, the Moroccans knew that safety lay in a variety of interlocking obligations. That the ideal was not always achieved does not mean the entire system was vitiated. To the contrary, it means that it was as against that ideal that actual relationships were to be measured.

In the American West, states' water laws have not remained unchanged. But some of the changes point up the absence of the ameliorating elements of the regime borrowed from Morocco. So, for example, in the view of some scholars American court cases have all but eliminated the emphasis on prior appropriation, allowing controls from the central authority to displace the order of access. While other analysts argue that the system is still alive but seriously unwell, the lessons of more localized versions of the system first imported from Morocco remain to be considered. This is especially true of the acequia systems (from the Arabic *saquia*, or irrigation canal) found mainly among Hispanic users in the American Southwest that continue to exhibit both success and the features of flexibility and social integration that are at the heart of these systems.[8]

While large-scale irrigation systems were not uncommon in North Africa and the Middle East, and centralized control—particularly for the supply of water to cities and large farms—has existed for centuries, the foundational principles of the Moroccan system are far from irrelevant even for large enterprises. Indeed, one could argue that the American penchant for solving problems with technology and a rights-based vision of water as property without the underlying culture of social involvement lie no less at the heart of the current crisis in Western water law than environmental factors alone. Unlike their North African progenitors, Americans are not, of course, suddenly going to form marital bonds across complementary ecological zones or fashion religious rituals through which goods are redistributed from the fortuitously plentiful to the momentarily deprived. But that does not mean Americans have only ownership rights and technology to rely upon. To the contrary, the social implications lost in the American adoption of Moroccan water law can be addressed through analogous mechanisms.

So, for example, beneficial use should not mean *any* use: the vast amount of water needed to raise alfalfa for cattle feed or almonds for export may have to be cut back, balanced with community-based decisions for temporary relief of the affected farmers and ranchers.[9] The Supreme Court has allowed the taking of property even by private enterprises for collective benefit.[10] Thus, appropriating groundwater to help localities whose wells have gone dry might be temporarily necessary, but it can be accompanied by forming mutual aid associations managed by all parties. And just as the local Moroccan water manager, based on reputation and community ties, is granted discretion to vary the rules when needed, so, too, tapping the knowledge and experience of well-regarded local citizens may safeguard fairness better than reliance on distant rule makers with only an indirect stake in the outcome.

A second principle was best articulated by the Nobel Prize–winning economist Elinor Ostrom, who showed that, if the appropriate level of trust is formed in a community, individuals will cooperate to preserve their common resource but that such trust requires ongoing face-to-face interaction and a highly decentralized political system—precisely the features the Moroccans stressed.[11] A corollary of trust—rather than its counter—is the pressure of public opinion. As Ostrom herself noted in an interview: "A lot of communities have figured out subtle ways of making everyone contribute, because if they don't, those who don't contribute are noticeable."[12] Interestingly, much of the success of water distribution in the past has, in fact, been the result of highly localized water districts controlling their own allocations.[13] But if trust and face-to-face communication are vital, the tendency for a kind of scale creep—in which the units that deal with distribution become ever larger in a typically American form of governmental centralization and bigger-is-better mentality that propels the system to ever more embracing levels of control—needs to be reversed, with management scaled down as much as possible to the interpersonal level. Thus if the units that deal with water in the American West are broken down into small enough groupings for communication and opinion to be effective, and if those foundational units are ratcheted up to workably larger ones only for limited purposes the lessons that generations of North Africans and others have learned about, communication may have a chance to yield self-restraint and limitations that are essential to the preservation of the commons.[14]

Water may be limited, but that may actually contribute to localized management. Scarcity does not merely test our technical and legalistic skills but also our ability to create civility. The three stories that began this chapter—in which the rules serve relationships, flexibility depends on local knowledge, and the transplanting of a legal system requires more than mere uprooting—all suggest that groupings of a workable size can be scaled up if the ethos they embody is not replaced with faceless forms of organization. Maybe, having learned how to manage a watercourse from the North Africans, we need to remember the rest of their lesson: Water is really about relationships, and property regimes cast up as God-given entitlements can never fully resolve shortages absent the ongoing creation of bonds of affinity and mutual regard. Americans may still say that "whiskey is for drinking and water is for fighting." But the Moroccans knew that water was really about each other: "Tell me, Sunken Well," asks the far-seeing Arab poet, "where are they who drank from you on summer days?" Americans, running short of more than water, may need to ask the same question.

8

The Prudent Investor Rule and the Duty to Community

How does one assess a fiduciary duty? Should it be goal-oriented, and, if so, is the goal solely one of pecuniary gain? Is it the fulfillment of a lofty purpose, even the approximation of an ideal? Is the requisite duty simply to provide the wherewithal necessary for the beneficiary to be able to make his or her own choices? Or to put it somewhat differently, is the result more important than the process of collective involvement in setting priorities?

Colleges and universities—perhaps like many other nonprofit or charitable organizations—cannot achieve their proffered ends if they do not have the necessary resources. But as in any such case, the balance of risk and reward is linked to both the ends to be sought and the principles that are to be maintained in the quest. As the ends vary, so may the means. If, for example, one is seeking to enroll more low-income students, funds for scholarships may have to be produced from investments more than from tuition fees; if the goal is to produce faculty research, the costs of such an enterprise may outweigh what fees alone can sustain. The problem, then, is one of creating the right mix within an overarching legal and cultural scheme that protects the assets and purposes alike.

The administration of college endowments is at once a special case and a typical one inasmuch as it forces us to think how best to govern the governors no less than how to formulate policies that allow them the scope for achieving collective ends. It also affords an opportunity to consider how local culture and values when brought into the law affect a given community. That the marketplace does not remain either constant or predictable only complicates the matter.

* * *

Do what you will, the capital is at hazard.
Justice Samuel Putnam, *Harvard College v. Amory*[1]

American colleges and universities are, understandably, deeply invested in the financial markets. The results of their involvement have, however, been uneven. During portions of the twenty-first century most have had a number of extremely good years: Princeton recorded a 46.9 percent gain in 2020–2021, Stanford gained 40.1 percent, and Washington University 65 percent.[2] But the bad years have been very bad indeed. In 2009–2010 many colleges saw their endowments decline by as much as 30 percent, with their investment income declining even more: Harvard's endowment dropped from $37 billion to $26 billion in 2009. The Harvard treasurer Jim Rothenberg acknowledged that, in 2008–2009, "Beyond the $11B decline in the value of the endowment, the University also had a loss of approximately $1.8 billion in investments made alongside the endowment, and a loss of $500 million realized in connection with our interest rate exchange agreements. All of these losses were a function of last year's extraordinary market conditions."[3] In other years losses may have been more moderate but not insignificant: in 2020–2021 Stanford lost 4.2 percent, Brown 4.6 percent, and MIT 5.3 percent.[4] Similarly, in fiscal year 2022 the median loss for college endowments was 10.2 percent, with only a handful barely in positive territory, the 27 percent gain in the S&P 500 index of 2021 having been followed by a 19.4 percent loss the next year.[5] In fiscal year 2023 Yale returned just 1.8 percent, Penn 1.3 percent, Bowdoin 1.6 percent, MIT -2.9 percent, Duke -1 percent, and Stanford 4.4 percent.[6] Investment in illiquid assets proved particularly burdensome in 2008 while losses in the technology sector were staggering to both investors and the ultra-rich founders of many of those companies, all of which affected alumni giving.[7] In poor years, such as 2008, staff members have lost jobs, student fees have escalated, and parents have had their financial planning severely disrupted.[8] Much of the loss may have been caused by debatable investment practices. The question thus arises whether colleges have violated what is commonly known as the "prudent investor rule."

Colleges, like other institutions that operate in a trust relationship, have long been expected to invest in a reasonably conservative way. The Massachusetts Rule, first articulated in 1830 in a Harvard University case, suggested that trustees must "observe how men of prudence, discretion, and intelligence manage their own affairs," taking both "probable income" and "probable safety" into consideration.[9] In more recent decades, however, laws modeled on the Uniform Prudent Investor Act of 1992 and adopted by almost all states have significantly altered the prudent investor rule.[10] Now, diversification is virtually required, unless there is reason to invest otherwise, and references to prohibited "speculation" have been replaced by an emphasis on the risk tolerance appropriate to each trust.[11]

Moreover, the delegation of investing to professionals is not only encouraged but also may be regarded as a duty. While risk is left undefined, and we no longer follow the nineteenth-century practice of permitting only those investments registered on an acceptable list, we do know that certain practices are still unacceptable. Colleges may not, for example, buy lottery tickets, since the chance of losing is simply too great. One court, faulting the practice of investing only in the S&P 500 index, required trustees to restore an estate to what it would have been if they had invested prudently.[12] Similarly, selective diversification and total delegation are likely to be regarded as lacking in prudence.

College trustees, of course, seldom exercise investment control directly. Some institutions have established separate investment companies that handle all decisions, whereas others run a portion of their investments internally and assign the remainder to outside managers.[13] The law requires exercising "due care" in selecting, instructing, and monitoring agents but is silent on how much trustees must understand about their institution's actual investments. Whether it is fair to expect college officers to understand the algorithms of, say, third-order derivatives, or to grasp the daily nuances of credit default swap insurance, statutes adopted by most states require trustees to be personally involved in the investment strategy and its oversight. Thus it is an open question whether trustees meet this standard if they do not make adequate efforts to understand the risks of these complex investment instruments.[14]

Naturally, college officials offer many reasons when there is a sharp decline in their endowments, often claiming, as a Harvard financial officer told the *Harvard Gazette*, that someone else had "ultimate financial responsibility." Explanations for their poor performance usually fall into several categories:

Everyone was doing it. Not since I tried that one on my second-grade teacher and received a look I will never forget would I commend this as a workable excuse. Doing one more deal because everyone else is doing them, particularly when history shows how easily the entire system can become destabilized, hardly seems consonant with responsible investing. To be told that "prudent" means "reasonable," and, as Yale Law School professor John Langbein notes, that "reasonable" in turn means the usual ways in which other trustees operate, may suit the lawyers and professors who drafted the rule.[15] But doing it just because others do it still would not pass muster with my second-grade teacher.

We did very well for many years. In many years, of course, endowments have benefited handsomely from their investment policies. Harvard had an annual return of 14.3 percent from 1990 to 2008, Princeton averaged 12.2 percent annually from 2012 to 2022, and many others approached or exceeded yearly double-digit gains. Reliance on modern portfolio theory, however, often seemed to promise more than it could deliver. Not only were the Dow and S&P 500 indexes lower in 2009 than a decade earlier but, as the legal scholar Stewart E. Sterk has pointed out, greater immunization of trustee liability only encouraged greater trustee risk-taking.[16]

Not all analysts agree. In a detailed study of investor behavior before and after the introduction of the modern prudent investor rule, two law professors argued that measures taken to balance portfolios were sufficient to inspire confidence:

> After enactment of the rule, trustees increased stockholdings in the relatively more risk-tolerant trusts and also increased rebalancing to manage the resulting increase in exposure to market risk. For those who believe that modern portfolio theory is an appropriate benchmark for trust investment management, these findings are comforting. The assumption of failed risk management by trustees that motivates recent calls for repeal or reform of the rule is inconsistent with the evidence on trust practice examined in this study.[17]

But "rebalancing," to use the authors' term, still involves choices and risks, and even if the long-term record remains impressive, considerable harm can occur when severe declines occur along the road. Indeed, risk-taking has not diminished in the period since the market lows of the Great Recession of 2008–2009. A survey by Russell Investments, a pension consulting firm, found that 58 percent of institutional investors had not changed their fundamental philosophy and that many were actually *increasing* by 5 percent their investments in the same instruments that had gotten them in trouble earlier.[18] Investment strategies based on the latest Nobel Prize in Economics may work for a time, but one is reminded of what the man who jumped off the roof said as he passed the second floor: "So far, so good." Again, the proof of prudent investing is not solely in the results but also in the appropriateness of the risks taken to achieve them.

The level of risk was appropriate to institutional needs and purposes. Many colleges were able to offer more scholarships, research support, improved facilities, and smaller classes when endowment returns were high. But if tolerance for risk is connected to the main purpose of the trust, then colleges may, for example, need to reconsider whether constant increases in administrative staff are always necessary. (For 16,937 students, Stanford lists 2,288 faculty and 15,750 administrative staff.) Cannot a decent university president be found for less than a salary of a million dollars or more? (Penn's Amy Gutmann, for example, received $3,164,829 in 2021 and $3.9 million in 2016, twenty times the median salary of Penn professors.)[19] If held to a meaningful interpretation of risk under the prudent investor rule, colleges might have to reconsider their priorities.

Even the professionals got it wrong. We all know examples: Long-Term Capital Management, a highly leveraged hedge fund set up by two Nobel Prize–winning economists, failed; Lehman Brothers Holdings Inc. was leveraged to the point that a small downward movement in the property market wiped it out. As the political philosopher John Gray has written, much of the underlying free-market theory took hold in the 1990s, "when economists came to believe that complex mathematical formulae could tame uncertainty in the murky world of derivatives."[20] Colleges, as John Cassidy notes, were caught up in an environment in which the operative theory was that "self-interest plus competition equals nirvana."[21]

But not everyone failed to see the handwriting on the wall. Several people were forced out of Lehman Brothers when they warned of the impending crisis. And Iris Mack, an investment analyst at Harvard, was fired after warning Lawrence H. Summers, Harvard's president at the time, of the risks of the university's strategy.[22] There is also no indication that lessons have been learned from the experience of 2008. As one commenter has demonstrated, universities have learned little from the financial crisis and are more invested in illiquid, nontransparent assets than before the financial crisis. That analyst concludes his article by recommending the establishment of board-level risk management committees to evaluate endowment investing policies.[23]

There may, however, be an even more important sociological factor at work in this process, one that might be referred to as the "culture of complicity." A powerful group may entice others into its practices so that the latter can neither extricate themselves without loss of stature nor blame others for what they are doing. As the governing boards of colleges have become dominated by business executives and investment bankers, and as college presidents are paid higher and higher salaries, the air of complicity has come to resonate with the title of a popular 1960s book, *I'm OK, You're OK*. An athletic coach with a highly fluctuating record may not be retained. Yet that has not usually been the case with administrators who make financial decisions. At a time when "accountability" is the watchword of the American public, colleges' involvement in the culture of complicity helps explain their unwillingness to accept blame. It is just unfortunate that, along with their corporate culture-mates, they have so far escaped any such accountability.[24]

Transparency, too, is not always up to the mark. A recent report by the Center for Social Philanthropy in Boston documents the prominence and potential conflicts of interest of financial professionals serving on the boards of six major colleges in New England. But even if there is no direct conflict of interest, one may still ask whether a trustee is acting solely in the interests of the institution if he or she is caught up in what the Center calls "the cult of the chief investment officer." Justice Louis D. Brandeis once said that "a lawyer who has not studied economics and sociology is very apt to become a public enemy." It may also be true that those who fail to take note of their college's involvement in the culture of complicity become equally complicit in its fiduciary risk.

No one wants to return to an era when delegation and diversification were impermissible. And rules should not be constructed simply as a function of any one moment in the markets. But one may fairly ask whether a given institution has, in fact, used the care, skill, and caution required by the prudent investor rule in choosing its investment professionals and whether trustees have ignored warnings about their agents' decisions. This is also true, for example, for donors who have made contributions to a college in return for an annuity, only to find that their money has been merged with other endowment funds and now produces far less income as a result of the college's risky investment strategy.

Given the legal requirement that risks be appropriate to purpose, one may even ask whether college endowments, notwithstanding their long-term horizon, can ever bear a substantial portion of their assets being committed to volatile investments. Statutes could, of course, be rewritten to limit the portion of trust investment in risky instruments or to impose a greater obligation to assess beneficiaries' needs. Because it could take a generation for new changes to be made in the statutes that govern trusts, however, the courts may be the only authority capable of clarifying the responsibilities of college officers in light of changing circumstances and theories. Indeed, the prudent investor rule may be interpreted to require a greater quest for information and greater oversight of those responsible for an institution's financial well-being. Although remedies like trustee reimbursement or removal may be sought, obtaining judicial clarification of an otherwise vague statute and achieving greater investment transparency for colleges may be the litigation goals most worth pursuing.

The history of *dis*investment is also relevant here. Many university boards refused to disinvest in South Africa at the time of apartheid, just as many have refused or have been reluctant to disinvest in fossil-fuel corporations or those lacking credible climate change programs. Only the actions of members of their own communities not otherwise represented at the investment table have led to change in a number of these policies. Clearly, direct involvement at every stage of investing by community representatives is impractical. But equally clearly, community involvement in investment policies can not only stimulate collective solidarity but also reflect more appropriately the thinking of a broad range of those affected by such decisions. Failure to consider nonmonetary repercussions of investment policy may serve as grounds for legal action against trustees; therefore the purposes of the trust and its goals should be clearly indicated from the outset.[25]

Indeed, greater involvement of the communities most affected by investment policies is consistent with the aims of prudent investing. Most institutions, whether through their board of governors or a select investment committee, profess to incorporate such broad-scale community involvement. But far more often than not this is mere window dressing. While representatives of students, parents, nonacademic staff, and others may be told they lack the expertise for investment or that too many cooks spoil the broth, the overall goal can incorporate wide-ranging representation, with actual investment decisions following from that premise. If, to reprise an earlier point, the priority is to get full funding for a limited number of enrollees, then the investment strategy might differ from one that is aimed at increasing *Newsweek* ratings through boosting criteria that the institution's full range of participants do not share. Representative members of the broader university community can engage in regular consultation with the investment professionals as part of the process of balancing risks and goals. While no system will be perfect, attending to the broader culture of the affected community could breathe distinct meaning into the miasma of the prudent investor rule and suffuse it with the form of prudential investment consonant with the desires of those whose lives are entwined with its repercussions.[26]

In the course of their testimony before Congress, several recent nominees to the Supreme Court referred to the proper role of the judge as that of an umpire. What Aristotle, who first made the analogy, actually said was that "the umpire has regard to equity, the judge to law." And we all know about the baseball umpire who, contrary to colleagues who claim to see them as they really are, says, "There's balls and there's strikes, and they ain't nothin' 'til I calls 'em." Like players and fans, however, those affected by decisions involving colleges' investments will not know if the prudent investor rule has been violated until the call is made. The players are not the only ones who count. Perhaps, in the name of meaningful accountability and community reinforcement, it is time that some of those who have borne the burden of their colleges' investment practices got the umpire back in the game.

Epilogue

*If I paint a wild horse, you might not see the horse, but you
will see the wildness.*
Pablo Picasso

Community, in the American imaginary, may reveal more than it
hides. It may show a people's self-image (however much the image
masks the self); it may reveal a middle path between persons and col-
lectives (while hiding the ambivalence felt toward each). Being too
exact, however, might only exacerbate the dilemma: The force of a
concept, a symbol, an idiom may lie in its imprecision, and like a
memory or a Wittgensteinian utterance we may need to appraise its
reality more in its traces than in its rarified essence. Held up as a
reflection of a hoped-for truth, trafficked among contenders for control of an elusive identity, the idea that out there lies a community
where one is at home may signify a path desired, yet a path marked
by the ineluctable tension between the personal struggle for vitalizing
categories and the communal impulse to retain order. The result is
neither an approach to vagueness nor one of utter solidity: like many
of the other concepts that guide our lives, "community" is no less real
for being as ghostly as it is palpable.

To bring culture into an understanding of the place of community
and group rights in the law is neither to replace law with anthropology nor to suggest that discretion and political considerations would
or should be eliminated in the process. That American constitutional
law should employ concepts like liberty or due process in ways that are
open-textured does not vitiate the argument that consideration of the
systemic reach of culture in one's legal affairs can at least be grounded
in a better understanding of culture itself. For if what we are referring
to is a view of humankind creating its own categories of experience and
proliferating those features across multiple domains, then attending to

the traces of that process may give somewhat greater substance to otherwise imprecise concepts.

We have seen, for example, that "tradition" can be formulated in terms of its semantic and associative impacts across domains rather than in its perceived scope or duration alone, that uncertainty is not indecision, or that the value of native peoples' productions is describable only in market terms. We have seen, too, that communities can be more involved at a face-to-face level for irrigation, investment, or determining when collective defamation has occurred without undermining the concepts of probability, prudence, or privacy. Indeed, as we have suggested, judges need not pretend to unwarranted certainty by bringing culture more fully into their considerations, but they risk a portion of their legitimacy when they fail to do so in a credible manner.

American courts face a crisis of legitimacy at the present time, their decisions often appearing to be grounded more on the personal, religious, or political views of their members than on a willingness to rule against their own beliefs. In so heterogeneous a society as that of the United States, one can no more point to uniform orientations in law than in politics. But legitimacy lies, in no small part, in the method of analysis, the style of discourse, and the canons of reasoning, not in results alone. And if courts attend in appropriate cases to the symbols and artifacts of what is shared—even if to no more than a level of passing acquaintance—they may be better able to maintain the conversation so vital to democracy and any felt sense of community. We are creatures of culture, and culture suffuses our legal decisions. Thinking carefully about how to theorize culture and how best to bring it more fully into the law can undoubtedly yield both greater legitimacy for the deciders and greater familiarity for those who must follow their decisions.

"Man," wrote Clifford Geertz, "is an animal suspended in webs of significance he himself has spun." Indeed, human beings are particularists more than universalists, creating new distinctions more often than new generalizations. The idea that we will all somehow become the same, that the world is becoming flat, that history has come to an end, or that global uniformity is our destiny is, as Margaret Chase Smith said long ago, "globaloney." Rather, what Werner Heisenberg said about quantum particles may, metaphorically, apply as well to cultural creations—that they are not exactly real: "[T]hey form a world of potentialities or possibilities rather than one of things or facts," excitations of the larger field of which they are the palpable avatar. Indeed, in the words of the linguist John McWhorter, it is commonly the case that "one can be massively fulfilled by language one doesn't fully comprehend." As in so many other domains of human life, references to "the community" may seem elusive, but it is no less true that in this instance the real is indeed as imagined as it is imaginary. At the end of the day we humans are category-creating critters, and denying, evading, or repressing that nature can only mislead us as, together and alone, we spin those webs of significance that are neither ensnaring nor unconstrained but, wavering tenaciously in the fickle breeze, portend our evanescent possibilities.

ACKNOWLEDGMENTS

This volume owes much of its stimulus to the colleagues and students with whom I have discussed these issues over the course of many years. I am especially grateful to my students at Princeton University and Columbia Law School for always keeping me aware of alternative interpretations and thought-provoking ideas.

Portions of the book were written while I was a senior fellow at Harvard Law School; others were first planned while a visitor at the Institute for Advanced Study, Princeton. I am sincerely grateful for the hospitality each of these institutions accorded me.

Excerpts of several chapters are reprinted by agreement with the following: *University of Chicago Law Review* (Introduction); *Encyclopedia of Law and Society* (Chapter 4); *NYU Journal of Legislation and Public Policy* (Chapter 6); and *The Chronicle of Higher Education* (Chapter 8).

The book is dedicated to my (truly great) great-nieces, Kaya Malika and Miriam.

NOTES

INTRODUCTION

1 Alexis de Tocqueville, *Democracy in America*, Harvey C. Mansfield and Delba Winthrop, trans. (Chicago: University of Chicago Press, 2000), 482.

2 *Id.*, 484.

3 *Id.*, 485.

4 *Id.*, 492.

5 *Id.*, 488, 491.

6 *Id.*, 491–92.

7 *Id.*, 485–92.

8 David Reisman, *The Lonely Crowd* (New Haven: Yale University Press, 1961); Robert Bellah et al., *Habits of the Heart* (New York: Harper & Row, 1986).

9 Sheila Limming, *Hanging Out: The Radical Power of Killing Time* (New York: Penguin, 2023).

10 Benedict Anderson, *Imagined Communities: Reflections on the Origin and Spread of Nationalism* (London: Verso, 1983). To some extent, of course, we all partake of imagined communities in the sense of believing that, even if we have only sporadic, purpose-driven contact with a particular category of others, we believe they can be precipitated for assistance, and this belief, if not always real, has its own real repercussions both psychologically and organizationally.

11 D. W. McMillan and D. M. Chavis, "Sense of Community: A Definition and Theory," *Journal of Community Psychology* 14, no. 1 (1986): 6–23, 16.

12 See, e.g., Michael Walzer, "The Communitarian Critique of Liberalism," *Political Theory* 18, no. 1 (February 1990): 6–23; Daniel Bell, "Communitarianism," *The Stanford Encyclopedia of Philosophy* (Fall 2022 ed.), Edward N. Zalta and Uri Nodelman, eds., https://plato.stanford.edu/archives/fall2022/entries/communitarianism.

13 For an argument that "community" is more often used to the advantage of the powerful than in the public interest, see Miranda Joseph, *Against the Romance of Community* (Minneapolis: University of Minnesota Press, 2002).

14 E. Galanter and M. Gerstenhaber, "On Thought: The Extrinsic Theory," *Psychological Review* 63, no. 4 (1956): 218–27, https://doi.org/10.1037/h0048568; Clifford Geertz, *The Interpretation of Cultures* (New York: Basic Books, 1973), 33–83; and Michael Newton, *Savage Girls and Wild Boys: A History of Feral Children* (London: Faber and Faber, 2002).

15 This overall interpretation of tribes is explored in detail in my forthcoming book *Why Tribal Lives Matter: Challenging the Image, Shifting the Paradigm*.

16 David Ignatius, *The Quantum Spy* (New York: Norton, 2017).

17 Albert O. Hirschman, *Development Projects Observed* (Washington, DC: Brookings Institution, 1967). Hirschman sees this factor as varying when he adds that "in certain societies there is a systematic underestimate of one's own creativity."

18 Edward Levi, *An Introduction to Legal Reasoning*, rev. ed. (Chicago: University of Chicago Press, 1962).

19 Notwithstanding some use of mediation, this appears to be especially true of Western legal systems, whereas many other regimes—those of many indigenous peoples, Islamic law, etc.—focus on the restoration of relationships rather than the application of impersonal rules.

20 John Dewey, "Logical Method and Law," *Cornell Law Review* 10, no. 1 (1924): 17–27, http://scholarship.law.cornell.edu/clr/vol10/iss1/2.

21 Kenneth Weisbrode, *On Ambivalence* (Cambridge, MA: MIT Press, 2012), 68.

22 Justice Elena Kagan may say of the Supreme Court "we are all textualists now," but even the conservative Justices hardly ignore public opinion. See Harvard Law School, *The Antonin Scalia Lecture Series: A Dialogue with Justice Elena Kagan on the Reading of Statutes*, YouTube (November 25, 2015), www.youtube.com/watch?v=dpEtszFToTg. Thus, in *Bostock v. Clayton County, Georgia*, 140 S. Ct. 1731, 590 U.S. ___ (2020), holding that the Civil Rights Act's reference to "sex" includes sexual orientation and gender identity, the 6–3 majority opinion of Justice Neil Gorsuch, for all its originalist orientation, provoked Justice Samuel Alito to claim: "The court's opinion is like a pirate ship. It sails under a textualist flag, but what it actually represents is a theory of statutory interpretation that Justice Scalia excoriated—the theory that courts should 'update' old statutes so that they better reflect the current values of society." Gorsuch countered by citing a 1998 case in which Justice Antonin Scalia had written that a statutory prohibition can often go beyond "the principal evil" to cover reasonably comparable evils (citing *Oncale v. Sundowner Offshore Services, Inc.*, 523 U.S. 75, 79 (1998)).

1. IDENTIFYING THE INDEFINABLE

1 On these two aspects of tradition, see Eugenia Shanklin, "Two Meanings and Use of Tradition," *Journal of Anthropological Research* 37, no. 1 (Spring 1981): 71–89.

2 See, e.g., Eric Hobsbawm, *The Invention of Tradition* (Cambridge, UK: Cambridge University Press, 2004); Eric Hobsbawm and Terence Ranger, eds., *The Invention of Tradition* (Cambridge, UK: Cambridge University Press, 2012); and James R. Lewis and Olav Hammer, eds., *The Invention of Sacred Tradition* (Cambridge, UK: Cambridge University Press, 2008). For an example of a court crafting an historical pedigree because its own recent creation might appear to lack credibility, see Lee Cabatingan, "Time and Transcendence: Narrating Higher Authority at the Caribbean Court of Justice," *Law & Society Review* 50, no. 3 (2016): 674–702.

3 *Rochin v. California*, 342 U.S. 165, 169 (1952): quoting, in order, *Malinsky v. New York*, 324 U.S. 401, 416–17 (1945); *Snyder v. Massachusetts*, 291 U.S. 97, 105 (1934); and *Palko v. Connecticut*, 302 U.S. 319, 325 (1937). Also see the words of Justice John Marshall Harlan II, who, in his dissent in *Poe v. Ullman* (367 U.S. 497, 542 (1961)), wrote:

> Due process has not been reduced to any formula; its content cannot be determined by reference to any code. The best that can be said is that through the course of this Court's decisions it has represented the balance which our Nation, built upon postulates of respect for the liberty of the individual, has struck between that liberty and the demands of organized society. If the supplying of content to this Constitutional concept has of necessity been a rational process, it certainly has not been one where judges have felt free to roam where unguided speculation might take them. The balance of which I speak is the balance struck by this country, having regard to what history teaches are the traditions from which it developed as well as the traditions from which it broke. That tradition is a living thing. A decision of this Court which radically departs from it could not long survive, while a decision which builds on what has survived is likely to be sound. No formula could serve as a substitute, in this area, for judgment and restraint.

> In support of Justice Frankfurter and other judges who rely to some extent on their emotional reactions, see Paul Gewirtz, "On 'I Know It When I See It,'" *Yale Law Journal* 105, no. 4 (1996): 1023–47, 1032.

4 *Moore v. City of East Cleveland*, 431 U.S. 494, 503 (1977).

5 *Michael H. v. Gerald D.*, 491 U.S. 110 (1989).

6 Brennan continues:

> The pretense is seductive; it would be comforting to believe that a search for "tradition" involves nothing more idiosyncratic or complicated than poring through dusty volumes on American history. Yet, as Justice White observed in his dissent in *Moore v. East Cleveland*, 431 U.S. 494, 549 (1977): "What the deeply rooted traditions of the country are is arguable." Indeed, wherever I would begin to look for an interest "deeply rooted in the country's traditions," one thing is certain: I would not stop (as does the plurality) at Bracton, or Blackstone, or Kent, or even the American Law Reports in conducting my search. Because reasonable people can disagree about the content of particular traditions, and because they can disagree even about which traditions are relevant to the definition of "liberty," the plurality has not found the objective boundary that it seeks. *Michael H. v. Gerald D.*, 491 U.S. 110, 137 (1989).

> For further discussions of the legal concept of tradition, see also *Snyder v. Commonwealth of Massachusetts*, 291 U.S. 97, 105 (1934), and the cases cited therein.

7 *United States v. Virginia*, 518 U.S. 515, 569 (1996).

8 *Dobbs v. Jackson Women's Health Organization*, 142 S. Ct. 2228 (2022). The Second Amendment gun case is *New York State Rifle & Pistol Assn. v. Bruen*, 142 S. Ct.

2111 (2022). Examples of recent cases that repeatedly speak about "rights that are so rooted in the traditions and conscience of our people as to be ranked as fundamental" include: *McDonald v. City of Chicago*, 561 U.S. 742 (2010); *Kondrat'Yev v. City of Pensacola*, 949 F.3d 1319 (11th Cir. 2020); *Obergefell v. Hodges*, 576 U.S. 644 (2015); *Medina v. California*, 505 U.S. 437 (1992); and *Kahler v. Kansas*, 140 S. Ct. 1021 (2020). For the argument that tradition and history compel a different analysis of the Fifth Amendment's role in abortion issues, see Aaron Tang, "After *Dobbs*: History, Tradition, and the Uncertain Future of a Nationwide Abortion Ban," *Stanford Law Review* 75, no. 5 (2023): 1031–90.

9 *Bruen*, at 2127 (2022). For the argument against the historical test, see the petition for cert by Solicitor General Elizabeth Prelogar in *U.S. v. Rahimi*, www.supremecourt.gov/DocketPDF/22/22-915/259334/20230317174308399_Rahimi%20Pet%20-%20final.pdf.

10 *Id.*, at 2179.

11 *Rochin*, at 172.

12 *Id.*, at 170–71. Justice Frankfurter's reference to being "left at large" resonates with his correspondence with his close friend Judge Learned Hand, whose striking utterance "left at large as we are" in the case of *Repouille v. United States*, 165 F.2d 152 (2nd Cir. 1947). had a profound effect on Frankfurter. On *Repouille*, see Lawrence Rosen, *The Judgment of Culture* (London: Routledge, 2018), 1–14.

13 Compare the American "shocks the conscience" cases with several decisions from Canada employing the same concept: *Canada v. Schmidt*, [1987] 1 S.C.R. 500; *Serra v. Serra*, 2009 ONCA 105 (CanLII); and *Arndt v. Arndt*, 1991 CanLII 7240 (ONSC), aff'd (1993), 1993 CanLII 480 (Ont. C.A.).

14 2022 U.S. App. LEXIS 9913 (10th Cir. Ct. of App. 2022), internal citations omitted.

15 *Rochin*, at 172, citing *Hudson County Water Co. v. McCarter*, 209 U.S. 349, 355 (1908).

16 *Id.*, at 169.

17 *Id.*, at 179.

18 The reference here is to Justice Potter Stewart's famous remark about pornography: "I know it when I see it." *Jacobellis v. Ohio*, 378 U.S. 184, 197 (1964). See generally Gewirtz, "On 'I Know It When I See It.'"

19 Quoted in John P. Dawson, *The Oracles of the Law* (Ann Arbor: University of Michigan Law School, 1968), 128.

20 *Id.*, 417–19.

21 See, e.g., the sources discussed in Kunal M. Parker, "Context in History and Law: A Study of the Late Nineteenth-Century American Jurisprudence of Custom," *Law and History Review* 24, no. 3 (Fall 2006): 473–518. As for the professed neutrality of economic approaches, even the federal appellate court judge Richard Posner, the foremost exponent of applying economic analysis to the law, finally confessed: "'I pay very little attention to legal rules, statutes, constitutional provisions,' Judge Posner said. 'A case is just a dispute. The first thing you do is ask

yourself—forget about the law—what is a sensible resolution of this dispute?' The next thing, he said, was to see if a recent Supreme Court precedent or some other legal obstacle stood in the way of ruling in favor of that sensible resolution. 'And the answer is that's actually rarely the case,' he said. 'When you have a Supreme Court case or something similar, they're often extremely easy to get around.'" Adam Liptak, *"An Exit Interview with Richard Posner, Judicial Provocateur,"* New *York Times* (September 11, 2017). On the relation of rules to discretion, see especially Lorraine Daston, *Rules: A Short History of What We Live By* (Princeton, NJ: Princeton University Press, 2022).

22 On the role of custom in current tort law, see generally Steven Hetcher, "Creating Safe Social Norms in a Dangerous World," *Southern California Law Review* 73, no. 1 (1999–2000): 1–86.

23 Russell Kirk, *The Conservative Mind*, 7th ed. rev. (Washington, DC: Regnery Gateway, 2001), 7–10.

24 The key Brandeis brief was submitted in *Muller v. Oregon*, 208 U.S. 412 (1908).

25 On the idea of "thick description," see Clifford Geertz, *The Interpretation of Cultures: Selected Essays* (New York: Basic Books, 1973), 3–30.

26 Max Gluckman, *The Judicial Process Among the Barotse* (Manchester, UK: Manchester University Press, 1955), 20.

2. "LEFT AT LARGE"

1 *Rochin v. California*, 342 U.S. 165, 171–72 (1952) (Frankfurter, J., for the majority).

2 The current law is found at Code of Federal Regulations (CFR), Title 8, Chapter 1, Subchapter C, Part 316, § 316.10.

3 Quoted in Gerald Gunther, *Learned Hand: The Man and the Judge*, 2nd ed. (Oxford, UK: Oxford University Press, 2010), 544. For additional materials on the *Repouille* decision, see Lawrence Rosen, *The Judgment of Culture* (London: Routledge, 2018), 1–14.

4 M. de Voltaire (François-Marie Arouet), *Complete Works of Voltaire*, vol. 12, part 1 (Toronto: University of Toronto Press, 1968).

5 The fuller quote reads: "In our worship of certainty we must distinguish between the sound certainty and the sham, between what is gold and what is tinsel; and then, when certainty is attained, we must remember that it is not the only good; that we can buy it at too high a price; that there is danger in perpetual quiescence as well as in perpetual motion; and that a compromise must be found in a principle of growth." Benjamin Cardozo, *The Growth of the Law* (New Haven, CT: Yale University Press, 1924),17. Cardozo, in *The Nature of the Judicial Process* (New Haven, CT: Yale University Press, 1926, 165–66), also wrote:

I was much troubled in spirit, in my first years upon the bench, to find how trackless was the ocean on which I had embarked. I sought for certainty. I was oppressed and disheartened when I found that the quest for it was futile. I was trying to reach land, the solid land of fixed and settled rules, the paradise of a justice that would declare itself by tokens plainer and more commanding than its pale and glimmering reflections in my own vacillating mind and conscience.

6 H. L. A. Hart, *The Concept of Law*, 1st ed. (Oxford, UK: Oxford University Press, 1961), 125.

7 *Id.*, 119–20. See generally Imer Flores, "H. L. A. Hart's Moderate Indeterminacy Thesis Reconsidered: In Between Scylla and Charybdis?" *Problema: Anuario de Filosofía y Teoría del Derecho* 5 (2011): 127–73; reprinted as Georgetown Public Law and Legal Theory Research Paper No. 12–162, https://scholarship.law.george-town.edu/facpub/1116 and http://ssrn.com/abstract=2144929.

8 For a contrary view, see Shawn J. Bayern, "Against Certainty," *Hofstra Law Review* 41, no. 1 (2012): 53–90 ("many defenses of certainty in legal rules are tautological, irrelevant, or substantively overstated"). Even in business dealings a degree of uncertainty may be necessary as new methods and technologies work their way into understanding. John Dewey's admonition may, therefore, have general validity: he said that what may be required in the law is "a logic relative to consequences rather than to antecedents, a logic of prediction of probabilities rather than one of deduction of certainties." Dewey, "Logical Method and Law," *Cornell Law Review* 10, no. 1 (1924): 17–27, 26, http://scholarship.law.cornell.edu/clr/vol10/iss1/2.

9 See, e.g., Dan Simon, "On the Double-Consciousness of Judging: The Problematic Legacy of Cardozo," *Oregon Law Review* 79, no. 4 (2000): 1033–80.

10 Linda Greenhouse, *Becoming Justice Blackmun* (New York: Henry Holt and Co., 2005), 16.

11 *Id.*, 54–55.

12 *Id.*, 13.

13 *Id.*, 146.

14 *Furman v. Georgia*, 408 U.S. 238, 405 (1972). He continued: "I yield to no one in the depth of my distaste, antipathy, and, indeed, abhorrence, for the death penalty, with all its aspects of physical distress and fear and of moral judgment exercised by finite minds."

15 510 U.S. 1141, 1145 (1994) ("From this day forward, I no longer shall tinker with the machinery of death. For more than 20 years I have endeavored—indeed, I have struggled—along with a majority of this Court, to develop procedural and substantive rules that would lend more than the mere appearance of fairness to the death penalty endeavor. Rather than continue to coddle the Court's delusion that the desired level of fairness has been achieved and the need for regulation eviscerated, I feel morally and intellectually obligated simply to concede that the death penalty experiment has failed.")

16 *Herrera v. Collins*, 506 U.S. 390, 446 (1993). See also Greenhouse, *Becoming Justice Blackmun*, 175, 113–14.

17 J. Craig Crawford, "Blackmun's Solace—Religion 'Roe' Author Unfazed by Abortion Critics," *Orlando Sentinel*, October 14, 1990 ("Blackmun, who has served 30

years on the nation's highest court, is a lifelong Methodist who sometimes weeps with emotion during a church service.").

18 See www.umc.org/en/content/social-principles-the-nurturing-community#abortion On the Church's reaction to the decision in *Dobbs*, see Jim Patterson, "United Methodists React to End of Roe v. Wade," *UM News*, June 24, 2022, https://www.umnews.org/en/news/united-methodists-react-to-end-of-roe-v-wade. The Church's General Commission on the Status and Role of Women also issued the following statement under the title, "A Response of Lament to the SCOTUS Decision to Overturn Roe V. Wade":

> Today's Supreme Court decision to overturn Roe V. Wade creates gender, racial and economic injustice for all Americans. It draws deeper lines between those who have means and those who do not. It creates geographical disparities that erase equal access and opportunity to healthcare. By reducing a woman's rights, our class structure is further divided, contrary to our belief that all women and men are created equal. We grieve this injustice.

https://www.resourceumc.org/en/partners/gcsrw/home/content/a-response-of-lament-to-the-scotus-decision-to-overturn-roe-v-wade.

19 Greenhouse, *Becoming Justice Blackmun*, 137–38.

20 *Id.*, 207–8.

21 *Thornburgh v. American College of Obstetricians and Gynecologists*, 476 U.S. 747, 772 (1986). By contrast, Ruth Bader Ginsberg, who joined the Court in 1993, argued that, while it would be preferable to leave much about abortion to the legislature, any constitutional right to the procedure should be grounded in the Equal Protection Clause rather than in a penumbral right of privacy. See Aaron Blake, "What Ruth Ginsberg Really Said About *Roe v. Wade*," *Washington Post*, June 27, 2022.

22 Greenhouse, *Becoming Justice Blackmun*, 68.

23 *Id.*, 68.

24 *Id.*, 60.

25 *Id.*, 92.

26 *Id.*, 95. Of the two dissenters, Justice Byron White, who described himself as "liberal" on the question of abortion (*id.*, 94), argued that the court should not displace the state legislatures in this matter, while Justice (later Chief Justice) William Rehnquist argued in his opinion that the Fourteenth Amendment does not preclude the state from some forms of regulating abortion even in the first trimester. Neither dissent, therefore, was grounded in opposition to abortion per se. On the role of "quickening" in the common law, see the historians' amicus brief in *Dobbs*, www.supremecourt.gov/Docket-PDF/19/19-1392/192957/20210920133840569_19-1392%20bsac%20Historians.pdf.

27 See www.smu.edu/News/2013/antonin-scalia-dmn-29jan2013. Elsewhere Scalia says: "[T]he really significant and heartfelt issues are *all* resolved in the Constitution" (emphasis in original). Antonin Scalia, *Scalia Speaks* (New York: Crown Forum, 2017), 153.

28 Edmund S. Morgan, "Back to Basics," *New York Review of Books*, July 20, 2000.

29 See Erwin Chemerinsky, *Worse Than Nothing: The Dangerous Fallacy of Originalism* (New Haven: Yale University Press, 2022).

30 On the history of Catholic Supreme Court justices, see generally John T. Noonan, Jr., "The Catholic Justices of the United States Supreme Court," *Catholic Historical Review* 67, no. 3 (July 1981): 369–85.

31 Some commenters, of course, see a direct—and inappropriate—connection between a Justice's religious beliefs and his or her judicial decisions. Thus, the *New York Times* columnist Maureen Dowd flatly says of Justice Samuel Alito's majority opinion in *Dobbs*: "[T]his brazenly political justice who doesn't distinguish between his legal and religious views mercilessly stripped women of the right to make decisions about their bodies." Maureen Dowd, "Supremely Arrogant," *New York Times*, May 6, 2023. Others see the right-wing Catholic justices effecting their changes in the jurisprudence of religious freedom through the so-called shadow docket, whereby orders are issued without hearings, often when the public media are least likely to take note. See Stephen Vladeck, *The Shadow Docket: How the Supreme Court Uses Stealth to Amass Power and Undermine the Republic* (New York: Basic Books, 2023); and Linda Greenhouse, *Justice on the Brink: The Death of Ruth Bader Ginsburg, the Rise of Amy Coney Barrett, and Twelve Months That Transformed the Supreme Court* (New York: Random House, 2021).

32 Friedrich Hegel, *Daybreak: Thoughts on the Prejudices of Morality* (Cambridge, UK: Cambridge University Press, 1982).

33 *Veritatis Splendor*, Section 1, www.vatican.va/content/john-paul-ii/en/encyclicals/documents/hf_jp-ii_enc_06081993_veritatis-splendor.html.

34 *Id.*, Sections 1 and 4 (original italics).

35 Scalia, *Scalia Speaks*, 149 and 152.

36 *Id.*, 249.

37 See generally Steve Banner, *The Decline of Natural Law* (Oxford, UK: Oxford University Press, 2021); and Suzanna Sherry, "Natural Law in the States," *Cincinnati Law Review* 61, no. 1 (1992): 171–222. For supporting statements on the role judges have ascribed to natural law, including Justice Thomas's remarks at his confirmation hearing, see Lawrence Rosen, *The Judgment of Culture* (London: Routledge, 2018), 159–93.

38 On this, see my discussion in "'Borked': Judicial Temperament and the Quest for Certainty," in Lawrence Rosen, *The Crisis of Legitimacy* (London: Routledge, 2023), 11–31; and Robert H. Bork, *The Tempting of America* (New York: Free Press, 1997), 241–50. Bork subsequently converted to Catholicism and married a former nun. Among the reasons he gave for converting at age seventy-six were: "I found the evidence of the existence of God highly persuasive, as well as the arguments from design both at the macro level of the universe and the micro level of the cell. I found the evidence of design overwhelming, and also the number of witnesses to the Resurrection compelling. The Resurrection is established as a solid historical fact." Tim Drake, "Judge Bork Converts to the Catholic Faith," *Catholic Educa-*

tion Resource Center, 2003, www.catholiceducation.org/en/faith-and-character/faith-and-character/judge-bork-converts-to-the-catholic-faith.html. For examples of Catholic-based natural law philosophy, see Adrian Vermeule, *Common Good Constitutionalism* (Cambridge, UK: Polity Press, 2022); John Finnis, *Natural Law and Natural Rights*, 2nd ed. (Oxford, UK: Oxford University Press, 2011); and Robert P. George, *In Defense of Natural Law* (Oxford, UK: Clarendon Press, 1999).

39 See, e.g., the comments of the Harvard Law School professor Laurence Tribe in KK Ottesen, "Current Supreme Court is Damaging to the Country, Law Scholar Warns," *Washington Post*, August 16, 2022. ("The court has always been quite political. . . . The idea that judges could be apolitical doesn't make sense. . . . [Apropos *Dobbs*,] when anything can be overruled, precedent means nothing. And, when precedent means nothing, there is no longer a meaningful difference between the judiciary and the political branches. It's just who has the votes.")

40 Sean M. Kammer, "Reflections on Teaching Constitutional Law in the Midst of Constitutional Crisis," *South Dakota Law Review* 67, no. 2 (2022): 194–211.

41 Dahlia Lithwick, "What We Lose as John Roberts Is Sidelined on the Court," *Slate*, July 29, 2022.

42 Dewey, "Logical Method and Law," 24.

43 *United States v. State of Washington*, 384 F. Supp. 312 (W.D. Wash. 1974), aff'd, 520 F.2d 676 (9th Cir. 1975).

44 The absence of doubt need not, however, lead simply to intolerance of other perspectives. See generally Peter L. Berger and Anton C. Zijderveld, *In Praise of Doubt: How to Have Convictions Without Becoming a Fanatic* (New York: Harper-Collins, 2009).

45 National Opinion Research Center, "Most Catholic Americans disagree with hardline positions of church leadership," https://apnorc.org/projects/most-catholic-americans-disagree-with-hardline-positions-of-church-leadership.

46 Avishai Margalit, *On Compromise and Rotten Compromises* (Princeton, NJ: Princeton University Press, 2010), quoted in Kenneth Weisbrode, *On Ambivalence* (Cambridge, MA: MIT Press, 2012), 50.

47 Edward H. Levi, *An Introduction to Legal Reasoning*, 2nd ed. (Chicago: University of Chicago Press, 2013).

48 Thomas Kuhn, *The Structure of Scientific Revolutions* (50th anniversary edition) (Chicago: University of Chicago Press, 2012), 23. See also Leah Trueblood and Peter Hatfield, "Precedent and Paradigm: Thomas Kuhn on Science and the Common Law," in Timothy Endicott, Hafsteinn Dan Kristjánsson, and Sebastian Lewis, eds., *The Philosophical Foundations of Precedent* (Oxford, UK: Oxford University Press, 2023), Chapter 7, https://ssrn.com/abstract=4061076.

49 Weisbrode, *On Ambivalence*, 1.

50 Stanley Diamond, "Introductory Essay," in Paul Radin, *The Trickster* (New York: Philosophical Library, 1956), xxi.

51 "And as long as universals can be ambushed by unforeseen particulars, discretion will have to come to the rescue. The only question is whether it does so furtively

and secretly or openly, once again recognised and respected as a form of public reason." Lorraine Daston, "The Virtue of Discretion," *Aeon*, April 21, 2023; and Lorraine Daston, *Rules: A Short History of What We Live By* (Chicago: University of Chicago Press, 2022).

52 Oliver Wendell Holmes, Jr., "Natural Law," *Harvard Law Review* 32, no. 1 (November 1918): 40–44, 40. Elsewhere Holmes says: "The language of judicial decision is mainly the language of logic. And the logical method and form flatter that longing for certainty and for repose which is in every human mind. But certainty generally is an illusion." Oliver Wendell Holmes, Jr., *Collected Legal Papers* (New York: Harcourt, Brace and Co., 1921), 181. For a critique of Holmes on this point, see Dewey, "Logical Method and Law," 17–27.

53 Frederic R. Coudert, "Certainty and Justice," *Yale Law Journal* 14, no. 7 (May 1905): 361–73, 373.

54 Learned Hand's 1944 "Spirit of Liberty" speech is available at https://www.thefire.org/research-learn/spirit-liberty-speech-judge-learned-hand-1944.

55 Quoted in Ruth Marcus, "You Thought the Supreme Court's Last Term Was Bad? Brace Yourself," *Washington Post*, September 30, 2022.

3. ABORTION AND THE CONSTITUTIONAL PROTECTION OF DIVERSITY

1 *Dobbs v. Jackson Women's Health Organization*, 142 S. Ct. 2228 (2022).

2 On the litigation strategies that may have to be revised in the light of *Dobbs*, see David S. Cohen, Greer Donley, and Rachel Rebouché, "Rethinking Strategy After *Dobbs*," *Stanford Law Review Online* 75 (2022): 1ff.

3 See, e.g., Randy E. Barnett, ed., *Rights Retained By the People: The History and Meaning of the Ninth Amendment* (Fairfax, VA: George Mason University Press, 1990); Dan Farber, *Retained By the People: The "Silent" Ninth Amendment and the Constitutional Rights Americans Don't Know They Have* (New York: Basic Books, 2007); and Dan Farber "The Ninth Amendment and Individual Rights: A Reply to Professor McAffee," *Nevada Law Journal* 9 (2008): 243–44.

4 See Randy E. Barnett, "The Ninth Amendment: It Means What It Says," *Texas Law Review* 85, no. 1 (2006): 1–82. See also Thomas B. McAffee, "The Original Meaning of the Ninth Amendment," *Columbia Law Review* 90 (1990): 1215–1320. For the argument that the Founders, having adopted the common law as practiced in England, preserved through the Ninth Amendment that law's right to an abortion prior to the quickening of the fetus, see Damon Root, "Alito's Abortion Ruling Overturning *Roe* Is an Insult to the 9th Amendment," *Reason*, June 24, 2002, https://reason.com/2002/06/24/alitos-abortion-ruling-overturning-roe-is-an-insult-to-the-9th-amendment.

5 Robert H. Jackson, *The Supreme Court in the American System of Government* (Cambridge, MA: Harvard University Press, 1955).

6 *Griswold v. State of Connecticut*, 381 U.S. 479 (1965), Justice Goldberg (concurring, at 487): "[T]he language and history of the Ninth Amendment reveal that the

Framers of the Constitution believed that there are additional fundamental rights, protected from governmental infringement, which exist alongside those fundamental rights specifically mentioned in the first eight constitutional amendments"; Justice Stewart (dissenting, at 530): "[T]he idea that a federal court could ever use the Ninth Amendment to annul a law passed by the elected representatives of the people of the State of Connecticut would have caused James Madison no little wonder." During his failed confirmation hearing, Robert Bork famously characterized the Ninth Amendment as like an "inkblot" on the Constitution that may cover a meaning we cannot see and as to whose meaning we should not speculate. See generally Robert Bork, *The Tempting of America* (New York: Free Press, 1997), 183–85, 183 ("whatever purpose the Ninth Amendment was intended to serve, the creation of a mandate to invent constitutional rights was not one of them").

7   Barnett, "The Ninth Amendment," 29.

8   See, e.g., *United Public Workers v. Mitchell*, 330 U.S. 75, 94 (1947). ("We accept appellants' contention that the nature of political rights reserved to the people by the Ninth and Tenth Amendments are involved.") Neither in *Mitchell* nor in any other case has the Court relied mainly on the Ninth Amendment in a decision. As summarized by one commentor: "More than two centuries after its ratification, the Ninth Amendment has yet to constitute the primary basis of a single Supreme Court ruling." Tom Head, "Ninth Amendment Supreme Court Cases," *ThoughtCo*, July 29, 2021, thoughtco.com/ninth-amendment-supreme-court-cases-721170.

9   George Washington, *Washington's Farewell Address* (New York: New York Public Library, 1935), 3.

10 Marcus Tullius Cicero, *De Officiis*, Book 1, Section 56, Project Gutenberg, www.gutenberg.org/ebooks/47001.

11 25 United States Code (U.S.C.), Chapter 32, §§ 3001 et seq.

12 See www.youtube.com/watch?v=WrIn8qM-zvA for the oral arguments before the Supreme Court in *Students for Fair Admissions v. University of North Carolina* and *Students for Fair Admissions v. President and Fellows of Harvard College.*

13 See Hannah Natanson, "Are Book Bans Discrimination? Biden Administration to Test New Legal Theory," *Washington Post*, January 13, 2023.

14 *Bowers v. Hardwick*, 478 U.S. 186, 213 (1986). Also see the language of the lower court in *Students for Fair Admissions, Inc. v. President & Fellows of Harvard College*, 261 F. Supp. 3d 99 (D. Mass. 2017), and www.apa.org/about/offices/ogc/amicus/student-fair-admissions.pdf.

15 United Nations, Convention on Biological Diversity, Treaty Series 1760, 79, 1993.

16 United Nations, UNESCO Recommendation on Safeguarding of Traditional Culture and Folklore, Paris: UNESCO, 1989.

17 International Labor Organization Indigenous and Tribal Peoples Convention 1989 (No. 169).

18 United Nations, UNESCO, Universal Declaration on Cultural Diversity, Paris: UNESCO, 31 Session, 2001.

19 See generally Janet Blake, *International Cultural Heritage Law* (Oxford, UK: Oxford University Press, 2015), 194–229; and Francesco Francioni, "Beyond State Sovereignty: The Protection of Cultural Heritage as a Shared Interest of Humanity," *Michigan Journal of International Law* 25 (Summer 2004): 1209–28.

20 The Tenth Amendment reads: "The powers not delegated to the United States by the Constitution, nor prohibited by it to the States, are reserved to the States respectively, or to the people."

21 "To separate them from others of similar age and qualifications solely because of their race generates a feeling of inferiority as to their status in the community that may affect their hearts and minds in a way unlikely ever to be undone." *Brown v. Board of Education*, 347 U.S. 483, 494 (1954).

22 See generally Note, "Equal Dignity—Heeding Its Call," *Harvard Law Review* 132, no. 4 (2019): 1323–44; and Adeno Addis, "Justice Kennedy on Dignity," *Houston Law Review* 60 (2022–23), Tulane Public Law Research Paper No. 20–10, https://ssrn.com/abstract=3694014 or http://dx.doi.org/10.2139/ssrn.3694014.

23 For example, Section 34 of the Encyclical, entitled "An Attitude of Responsibility," reads:

> Man's personal dignity requires besides that he enjoy freedom and be able to make up his own mind when he acts. In his association with his fellows, therefore, there is every reason why his recognition of rights, observance of duties, and many-sided collaboration with other men, should be primarily a matter of his own personal decision. Each man should act on his own initiative, conviction, and sense of responsibility, not under the constant pressure of external coercion or enticement. There is nothing human about a society that is welded together by force. Far from encouraging, as it should, the attainment of man's progress and perfection, it is merely an obstacle to his freedom.

See www.vatican.va/content/john-xxiii/en/encyclicals/documents/hf_j-xxiii_enc_11041963_pacem.html.

24 The concept of dignity as legal entitlement is also becoming more central to international human rights law. See Ginevra Le Moli, *Human Dignity in International Law* (Cambridge, UK: Cambridge University Press, 2021).

25 *Obergefell v. Hodges*, 576 U.S. 644 (2015).

26 See https://fedsoc.org/commentary/publications/the-great-debate-justice-william-j-brennan-jr-october-12-1985 ("For the Constitution is a sublime oration on the dignity of man, a bold commitment by a people to the ideal of libertarian dignity protected through law."). In their discussion of how artificial intelligence could generate a less discriminatory result than what the authors believe to be Justice Alito's inappropriate decision in *Dobbs*, two law professors could similarly ask: "Why will the Supreme Court of the United States likely uphold a claim that a chatbot [a computer program that simulates human conversation] [should be] regarded (at least initially) as inconsistent with human dignity?" Michael C. Dorf

and Laurence H. Tribe, "Court v. Chatbot," *New York Review of Books*, December 26, 2022.

27 See, e.g., Vimal Patel, "A Lecturer Showed a Painting of the Prophet Muhammad: She Lost Her Job," *New York Times*, January 8, 2023.

28 Kenan Malik, "An Art Treasure Long Cherished by Muslims Is Deemed Offensive. But to Whom?" *The Guardian*, January 8, 2023.

29 Pope Francis, "To the Diplomatic Corps Accredited to the Holy See," January 2022, www.vatican.va/content/francesco/en/events/event.dir.html/content/vaticanevents/en/2022/1/10/corpo-diplomatico.html.

30 Hugo Grotius, *The Freedom of the Seas [Mare Liberum]*, James Brown Scott, ed., and Ralph Van Deman Magoffin, trans. (New York: Oxford University Press, 1916), 7.

4. GROUP DEFAMATION

1 See, e.g., Evan P. Schultz, "Group Rights, American Jews, and the Failure of Group Libel Law 1913–1952," *Brooklyn Law Review* 66, no. 1 (2017): 71–145; and James Jay Brown and Carl L. Stern, "Group Defamation in the U.S.A.," *Cleveland-Marshall Law Review* 13 (January 1964): 7–32.

2 On the latter resolutions, see L. Bennett Graham, "Defamation of Religions: The End of Pluralism?" *Emory International Law Review* 23, no. 1 (2009): 69–84.

3 Note, "Statutory Prohibition of Group Defamation," *Columbia Law Review* 47, no. 4 (May 1947): 595–613, 609–612. The *Columbia Law Review* statement builds on the essays by David Riesman, "Democracy and Defamation: Control of Group Libel," *Columbia Law Review* 42, no. 5 (May 1942): 727–80; "Democracy and Defamation: Fair Game and Fair Comment I," *Columbia Law Review*, 42, no. 7 (September 1942): 1085–1123; and "Democracy and Defamation: Fair Game and Fair Comment II," *Columbia Law Review* 42, no. 8 (1942): 1282–1318.

4 505 U.S. 377 (1992). By contrast, in *Virginia v. Black*, 538 U.S. 343 (2003), the Supreme Court, by a 5–4 vote, deemed constitutional part of a Virginia statute outlawing the public burning of a cross if done with an intent to intimidate, noting that such expression "has a long and pernicious history as a signal of impending violence." And while *Beauharnais v. Illinois*, 343 U.S. 250 (1952), has not been formally overturned, subsequent Supreme Court cases have largely not supported its 5–4 decision favoring laws like the Illinois statute that made it illegal to publish or exhibit any writing or picture portraying the "depravity, criminality, unchastity, or lack of virtue of a class of citizens of any race, color, creed or religion."

5 *Irving v. Penguin Books*, [2001] EWCA Civ. 1197, http://www.bailii.org/ew/cases/EWCA/Civ/2001/1197.html. See generally Deborah E. Lipstadt, *History on Trial: My Day in Court With a Holocaust Denier* (New York: Ecco, 2006).

6 See Thomas David Jones, "Human Rights: Freedom of Expression and Group Defamation under British, Canadian, Indian, Nigerian and United States Law—A Comparative Analysis," *Suffolk Transnational Law Review* 18, no. 2 (1995): 427–588.

7 See *UWM Post v. Board of Regents of University of Wisconsin*, 774 F. Supp. 1163 (E.D. Wis. 1991) ("the suppression of speech, even where the speech's content appears to have little value and great costs, amounts to governmental thought control"). See also *Dambrot v. Central Michigan University*, 55 F.3d 1177 (6th Cir. 1995); and *Corry v. Stanford*, No. 740309 (Cal. Super. Ct., February 27, 1995).

8 American Law Institute, *Restatement (Second) of Torts*, § 564A, 1977.

9 On this "intensity of suspicion" test and related issues, see Jeffrey Greenwood, "Group Defamation, Power, and a New Test for Determining Plaintiff Eligibility," *Fordham Intellectual Property, Media & Entertainment Law Journal* 28, no. 4 (2018): 871–945, https://ir.lawnet.fordham.edu/iplj/vol28/iss4/4.

10 Brown and Stern, "Group Defamation in the U.S.A.," 11.

11 In Greenwood's words: "The Intensity of Suspicion test provides flexibility and an evidentiary approach, while delivering inconsistent and constitutionally troubling results. The Restatement delivers a degree of consistency at the expense of flexibility and a reliance on arbitrary numerical guidelines." *Id.*, 918.

12 Kenneth Lasson, "Racial Defamation as Free Speech: Abusing the First Amendment," *Columbia Human Rights Law Review* 17, no. 1 (1985): 11–55, 54–55: "To believe that all ugly ideas wither when aired is the height of naivete. It casts contempt upon history. . . . Punishment of racial defamation has not jeopardized liberty elsewhere, nor would democracy in America suffer were bigots prohibited from promoting hatred on the public streets. . . . [R]acial extremism rests in the kind of fervently held beliefs, political thought, and 'truth' which freedom of speech was never designed to protect."

13 See Loren P. Beth, "Group Libel and Free Speech," *Minnesota Law Review* 39 (1955): 167–84, 182 ("group libel laws are unlikely to achieve any substantial result"). By comparison, it has been argued that "America's historical experiences indicate that group libel laws seem best suited to a conception of society that views group rights generally in favorable terms." Schultz, "Group Rights," 145.

14 On rare occasions there has been some recognition that communities possess cognizable rights, as in the concerns of an ethnic group whose community would be sundered by a major highway project or the Amish who do not wish to send their children to public school beyond the eighth grade. But even here the analogy or legal fiction focuses on the individual, in the former instance as an impediment to personal travel, in the latter as an interference with parental and individual religious rights. See generally Lawrence Rosen, *The Judgment of Culture* (London: Routledge, 2018), 227–46.

15 A British journalist suggests:

What makes a libel offensive is not so much the damage it does to this or that individual but the fact that it does so falsely. . . . A fair and powerful libel law must deal with and deter the publishing of lies. For it to be effective it needs an accessible and inexpensive tribunal to which people can complain when false statements are made about them. The tribunal should have the power to provide a remedy where such a remedy would be most effective in the publication concerned. It should be able to impose upon such publications corrections and apologies of much greater size and prominence than the original mistake. . . . As things stand, the libel law does not correct mistakes, and by and large does not (except in rare cases) restore falsely injured reputations. If libel became a law for correcting falsehoods and exposing malice, reputations could be quickly restored and the offending newspapers properly punished.

Paul Foot, "Bunfights," *London Review of Books* 13, no. 5 (March 7, 1991).

16 See, e.g., Nat Stern, "The Certainty Principle as Justification for the Group Defamation Rule," *Arizona State Law Journal* 40, no. 3 (Fall 2008): 951–1002, 970, n. 114 (analyzing commentary condemning defamation law as "confusing and even incoherent"). Even the question of what constitutes an "injury in fact" in a number of legal domains has been rendered unclear as a result of recent court rulings. See, e.g., *TransUnion LLC v. Ramirez*, 141 S. Ct. 2190 (2021) (holding that the mere risk of future harm does not suffice to confer Article III standing in a suit for damages). See also Cass Sunstein, "Injury in Fact, Transformed," in David A. Strauss et al., eds., *Supreme Court Review 2021* (Chicago: University of Chicago Press, 2022), 349–74.

17 Chief Justice Warren E. Burger, "The State of Justice," *ABA Journal* 70, no. 4 (April 1984): 62–66.

18 See, e.g., Alternative Dispute Resolution, 28 U.S.C. Chapter 44 (1998) and 28 U.S.C. § 651 (1998). Other legislation refers to specific ADR programs for different federal agencies. There may also be features to be considered from the experience with restorative justice programs, in which victims and perpetrators of a crime are brought together.

19 28 U.S.C. §§ 651 et seq., § 653 (emphasis added).

20 See, e.g., the Greensboro Truth and Reconciliation Commission, https://greensborotrc.org/exec_summary.pdf.

21 For an argument favoring group defamation laws notwithstanding the danger of overreach, see Hadley Arkes, "Civility and the Restriction of Speech: Rediscovering the Defamation of Groups," *The Supreme Court Review, 1974* (Chicago: University of Chicago Press, 1974), 281–335.

5. ADJUDICATING THE DISPOSITION OF INDIGENOUS REMAINS

1 See David Ives Bushnell, Jr., *Native Cemeteries and Forms of Burial East of the Mississippi* (Washington, DC: U.S. Government Printing Office, 1920); Douglas R. Mitchell and Judy L. Brunson-Hadley, eds., *Ancient Burial Practices in the American Southwest: Archaeology, Physical Anthropology, and Native American Perspectives* (Albuquerque: University of New Mexico Press, 2001); Richard White, *The Middle Ground: Indians, Empires, and Republics in the Great Lakes Region, 1650–1815* (New York: Cambridge University Press, 1991), 99–104. See generally Lawrence Rosen, "Burial Grounds, Native American," *International Encyclopedia*

of the Social Sciences, 2nd ed., vol. 1, Wm. A. Darity, Jr., ed. (Detroit: Macmillan Reference, 2008), 394–96.

2 See generally Sangita Chari and Jaime Lavellee, eds., *Accomplishing NAGPRA* (Corvallis: Oregon State University Press, 2013); Chip Colwell, *Plundered Skulls and Stolen Spirits* (Chicago: University of Chicago Press, 2019); Kathleen Fine-Dare, *Grave Injustice* (Lincoln: University of Nebraska Press, 2002); Devon Mihesuah, ed., *Repatriation Reader: Who Owns American Indian Remains?* (Lincoln: University of Nebraska Press, 2000); and Logan Jaffe, Mary Hudetz, and Ash Ngu, "Dozens of Universities and Museums Pledge to Return Native American Remains: Few Have Funded the Effort," *Pro Publica*, March 15, 2023. For the argument that the dead continue to possess constitutional rights, including the right not to be disturbed, see Fred O. Smith, Jr., "The Constitution After Death," *Columbia Law Review* 120 (2020): 1471–1548.

3 See David Hurst Thomas, *Skull Wars: Kennewick Man, Archaeology, and the Battle for Native American Identity* (New York: Basic Books, 2000).

4 *Bonnichsen v. United States* 367 F.3d 864 (9th Cir. Ct. of App. 2004).

5 On the contestable concept of "indigenous," see Manvir Singh, "It's Time to Rethink the Idea of the 'Indigenous,'" *The New Yorker*, February 20, 2023.

6 Anna Maria Ortiz, *Federal Agency Efforts and Challenges Repatriating Cultural Items*, GAO-22-105685 (February 2, 2022) 9, https://www.gao.gov/assets/720/718889.pdf. For statistics on the number of remains in the collections of various institutions, see Ash Ngu and Andrea Suozzo, "Does Your Local Museum or University Still Have Native American Remains?" *Pro Publica*, January 11, 2023, https://projects.propublica.org/repatriation-nagpra-database. On the decision by the American Museum of Natural History to remove skeletal remains from public displays, see Zachary Small, "Facing Scrutiny: A Museum that Holds 12,000 Human Remains Changes Course," *New York Times*, October 15, 2023.

7 Constant Méheut, "A Paris Museum Has 18,000 Skulls. It's Reluctant to Say Whose," *New York Times*, November 29, 2022.

8 Pub. L. 101–601, 25 U.S.C. §§ 3001 et seq., § 3013, provides that the United States district courts will have jurisdiction over any action alleging a violation of the statute and that the courts shall have the authority to issue such orders as may be necessary to enforce the statute. For examples of the exercise of such jurisdiction, see *Na Iwi O Na Kupuna O Mokapu (Na Iwi) v. Dalton*, 897 F. Supp. 1397 (D. Hawaii 1995), and *White v. Regents of the University of California*, 765 F.3d 1010 (2015). For an argument that NAGPRA should apply to a wide range of instances, see Alix Rogers, "Owning Geronimo but Not Elmer McCurdy: The Unique Property Status of Native American Remains," *Boston College Law Review* 60, no. 8 (2019): 2347–2408, https://lawdigitalcommons.bc.edu/bclr/vol60/iss8/4.

9 See, e.g., Note, "The Case for Special Juries in Complex Civil Litigation," *Yale Law Journal* 89 (1980): 1155–76.

10 H. L. A. Hart, *The Concept of Law* (Oxford, UK: Clarendon Press, 1961), 125.

11 See, e.g., *Lyng v. Northwest Indian Cemetery*, 485 U.S. 439 (1988).

12 About 45 percent of the claims received some compensation. For the argument that the ICC failed as a vehicle for doing justice to Indian claims, particularly since it could not award land, see Ward Churchill, "Charades, Anyone? The Indian Claims Commission in Context," *American Indian Culture & Research Journal* 24, issue 1 (2000): 43–68. See generally Harvey D. Rosenthal, *Their Day in Court: A History of the Indian Claims Commission* (New York: Garland Publishing, 1990).

13 See generally James Yaffe, *So Sue Me! The Story of a Community Court* (New York: Saturday Review Press, 1972); and Israel Goldstein and Simon Agranat, *Jewish Justice and Conciliation: History of the Jewish Conciliation Board of America, 1930–1968* (New York: Ktav, 1981).

14 For the Navajo example, see James W. Zion, "The Navajo Peacemaker Court: Deference to the Old and Accommodation to the New," *American Indian Law Review* 11 (1983): 89–109; for the Hopi, see Justin B. Richland, *Arguing with Tradition: The Language of Law in Hopi Tribal Court* (Chicago: University of Chicago Press, 2008).

15 See, e.g., Sabrina Imbler, "New DNA Analysis Supports an Unrecognized Tribe's Ancient Roots in California," *New York Times*, April 12, 2022. See generally Rachel Monroe, "The Bodies in the Cave," *The New Yorker*, October 10, 2022, 26–30; Jennifer Raff, *Origin: A Genetic History of the Americas* (New York: Twelve, 2022). For a summary of current thinking on the arrival of humans to the North American continent and its implications for contemporary native peoples, see Jennifer Raff, "Finding the First Americans," *Aeon*, December 22, 2022, https://aeon.co/essays/the-first-americans-a-story-of-wonderful-uncertain-science.

16 See, e.g., Anonymous, "Chukchansi Tribe Starts Disenrollment Proceedings Against More Than 60 Citizens," *Indians.com*, June 27, 2019, www.indianz.com/News/2019/06/27/chukchansi-tribe-starts-disenrollment-pr.asp; and Linda Geddes, "Tribal Wars," *New Scientist* 210, no. 2817 (June 15, 2011): 8–10.

17 See James L. Gibbs, "The Kpelle Moot," *Africa* 33, no. 1 (1963): 1–11.

18 See Lynn Berat, "The Role of Conciliation in the Japanese Legal System," *American University International Law Review* 8, no. 1 (1992): 125–54.

19 See, e.g., Lawrence Rosen, *The Justice of Islam* (Oxford, UK: Oxford University Press, 2000), chs. 5 and 7.

20 Vine Deloria, Jr., *Custer Died for Your Sins* (New York: Macmillan, 1969).

21 Joseph Raz, *Ethics in the Public Domain* (Oxford, UK: Oxford University Press, 1995), 174 and 189.

22 Michael Walzer, "The New Tribalism," *Dissent* (Spring 1992): 164–71, esp. 168 and 171.

23 Jeremy Waldron, "Minority Cultures and the Cosmopolitan Alternative," *University of Michigan Journal of Law Reform* 25, nos. 3–4 (1992): 751–93, 788 (emphasis in original). For further indications of his position, see Jeremy Waldron, "Superseding Historic Injustice," *Ethics* 103, no. 1 (1992): 4–28; and Jeremy Waldron, "Redressing Historic Injustice," *University of Toronto Law Journal* 5 (2002):

135–160. See also Kimberlee Weatherall, "Culture, Autonomy and *Djulibinyamurr*: Individual and Community in the Construction of Rights to Traditional Designs," *Modern Law Review* 64, no. 2 (March 2001): 215–42; and Kerstin Reibold, "Why Indigenous Land Rights Have Not Been Superseded—A Critical Application of Waldron's Theory of Supersession," *Critical Review of International Social and Political Philosophy*, December 9, 2019, www.tandfonline.com/doi/full/10.1080/136 98230.2019.1697842.

24 For critiques of Rawls's *Law of Peoples*, see Thomas W. Pogge, "The Incoherence between Rawls's Theories of Justice," *Fordham Law Review*, 72, no. 5 (2004): 1739–59; and Allen Buchanan, "Rawls's Law of Peoples: Rules for a Vanished Westphalian World," *Ethics* 110, no. 4 (July 2000): 697–721.

25 See generally Deborah L. Levi, "The Role of Apology in Mediation," *New York University Law Review* 72, no. 5 (November 1997): 1165–1209.

26 For further examples, see Lawrence Rosen, *The Judgment of Culture: Cultural Assumptions in American Law* (London: Routledge, 2018), 17–93.

27 See Yves Dezalay and Bryant Garth, *Dealing in Virtue: International Commercial Arbitration and the Construction of a Transnational Legal Order* (Chicago: University of Chicago Press, 1996).

28 See generally Jethro K. Lieberman, "Lessons from the Alternative Dispute Resolution Movement," *University of Chicago Law Review* 53 (1986): 424–39.

29 It is important to note that, especially in the North American case, many native peoples did not actually bury their dead. Practices included exposure to the elements, encasement of bones in clay vessels, and cremation. Tribes also divided and/or moved with some frequency, leaving their ancestors' remains behind. That fact alone, however, ought not to preclude claims for proper treatment of those predecessors' bodies. As Alfred Schutz noted, "Graves and reminiscences can neither be transferred nor conquered." *Alfred Schutz on Phenomenology and Social Relations* (Chicago: University of Chicago Press, 1970), 88.

30 On the levels of proof in common law versus continental systems, see Kevin M. Clermont and Emily Sherwin, "A Comparative View of Standards of Proof," *American Journal of Comparative Law* 50, no. 2 (Spring 2002): 243–75.

31 On the benefits of consultation with native representatives, see Lucas Ritchie, "Indian Burial Sites Unearthed: The Misapplication of the Native American Graves Protection and Repatriation Act," *Public Land and Resources Law Review* 26 (2005): 71–96.

6. VALUING NATIVE CULTURE

1 *Alice in Wonderland* (Chapter XI: "Who Stole the Tarts?"). Dr. Johnson was equally skeptical about setting a value on a life: "Among the many improvements made by the last centuries in human knowledge, may be numbered the exact calculations of the value of life; but whatever may be their use in traffic, they seem very little to have advanced morality. They have hitherto rather been applied to

the acquisition of money than of wisdom." Samuel Johnson, *Rambler #71* (November 20, 1750).

2 See generally Cass Sunstein, "What Price Is Right?" *New York Review of Books*, June 10, 2021, 27ff.

3 See, e.g., Yazid Ben Hounet, "Cent dromadaires et quelques arrangements: Notes sur la diya (prix du sang) et son application actuelle au Soudan et en Algérie," *Revue des Mondes Musulmans et de la Méditerranée*, no. 131 (2012): 203–21; and Daniel Pascoe, "Is Diya a Form of Clemency?" *Boston University International Law Journal* 34 (2016): 149–79. One may even ask whether tort law compensation does not act as a partial, if somewhat disguised, version of blood-money payment.

4 See Arzoo Osanloo, *Forgiveness Work: Mercy, Law, and Victims' Rights in Iran* (Princeton, NJ: Princeton University Press, 2020).

5 *Ex Parte Crow Dog*, 109 U.S. 556, 3 S. Ct. 396, 27 L. Ed. 1030 (1883). See generally Sidney L. Harring, *Crow Dog's Case: American Indian Sovereignty, Tribal Law, and United States Law in the Nineteenth Century* (Cambridge, UK: Cambridge University Press, 1994). The congressional action was first codified in 1886 as the Seven Major Crimes Act, U.S. Statutes at Large 23, Chapter 341, and is now embodied in 18 U.S.C. § 1153.

6 See, e.g., the New Guinea examples in Debbora Battaglia, "Retaining Reality: Some Practical Problems with Objects as Property," *Man*, N.S., 29, no. 3 (September 1994): 631–44; and Simon Harrison, "From Prestige Goods to Legacies: Property and the Objectification of Culture in Melanesia," *Comparative Studies in Society and History* 42, no. 3 (July 2000): 662–79.

7 "For example, in a focus group conducted to test alternative ways to estimate willingness to accept compensation for the environmental damage caused by the Exxon-Valdez oil spill, a young woman leaped to her feet and angrily shouted, 'You mean to say I've been raped and you think there is some amount of money that will make me feel it didn't happen?' Subsistence and barter-based indigenous peoples might well shout the same lamentation." Robert Snyder, Daniel Williams, and George Peterson, "Culture Loss and Sense of Place in Resource Valuation: Economics, Anthropology and Indigenous Cultures," in Svein Jentoft, Henry Minde, and Ragnar Nilsen, eds., *Indigenous Peoples: Resource Management and Global Rights* (Delft, The Netherlands: Eburon Academic Publishers, 2003), 107–23, 113.

8 On the preemption rights of neighbors, see A. A. Oba, "Islamic Law as Customary Law: The Changing Perspective in Nigeria," *International and Comparative Law Quarterly* 51 (2002): 817–50; A. Zubair, "Denying the Neighbour's Right of Preemption (Shufah)—A Proper Interpretation of Islamic Law? *Alkamawa v. Bello and Anor*," ([1998] 6 S.C.N.J. 127); and Farhat J. Ziadeh, "Shuf'ah: Origins and Modern Doctrine," *Cleveland State Law Review* 34, no. 1 (1985–86): 35–46. There is a common Arab saying, similar to that found in Proverbs 27:10, that "your neighbor who is nearby is more important than your kinsman who is far away."

9 See generally Davina Cooper, "Far Beyond 'The Early Morning Crowing of a Farmyard Cock': Revisiting the Place of Nuisance within Legal and Political Discourse," *Social & Legal Studies* 11, no. 1 (2002): 5–35.

10 For suggested modes of assessing valuation in the case of native peoples, see, e.g., Brian Burfitt, "Valuing Footsteps—Towards a Valuation Model of Indigenous Knowledge and Cultural Expression for the Sustainability of Indigenous People's Culture," *Journal of Intellectual Property Law and Practice* 9, no. 5 (2014): 383–88; Stephen B. Brush and Doreen Stabinsky, eds., *Valuing Local Knowledge: Indigenous People and Intellectual Property Rights* (Washington, DC: Island Press, 1996); Robert A. Simons, Rachel Malmgren, and Garrick Small, eds., *Indigenous Peoples and Real Estate Valuation* (New York: Springer 2008); J. Burton, "The Principles of Compensation in the Mining Industry," in S. Toft, ed., *Compensation for Resource Development in Papua New Guinea* (Port Moresby and Canberra: Law Reform Commission of Papua New Guinea and Resource Management in Asia and the Pacific, Research School of Pacific and Asian Studies, Australian National University, National Centre for Development Studies, 1997), 116–36; and Lester I. Yano, "Protection of the Ethnobiological Knowledge of Indigenous Peoples," *UCLA Law Review* 41 (1993): 443–86.

11 See *Chilkat Indian Village v. Johnson*, 870 F.2d 1469 (9th Cir. 1989), and *Chilkat Indian Village, IRA v. Johnson* (Chilkat Trial Court 1993), *Indian Law Reporter* 20 (1993), 6127 (tribal law against alienation of traditional cultural objects prevails even though object was inherited from the original artisan); and Heide Brandes, "'Like Gold to Us': Native American Nations Struggle to Protect Wild Rice," *Sierra*, August 26, 2019.

12 See generally Edward Lazarus, *Black Hills/White Justice: The Sioux Nation Versus the United States, 1775 to the Present* (New York: HarperCollins, 1991). See also the Indian Claims Commission Act, 25 U.S.C. §§ 70a–70q (Suppl. 1, 1958).

13 On the failure of such approaches see, e.g., William Fisher, "The Puzzle of Traditional Knowledge" *Duke Law Journal* 67 (2018): 1511–78; and Kathryn Moynihan, "How Navajo Nation v. Urban Outfitters Illustrates the Failure of Intellectual Property Law to Protect Native American Cultural Property," *Rutgers Race & the Law Review* 19 (2018): 51–76.

14 Whether past offenses justify the return of native objects or retention where all may have access to them is debatable. See, e.g., Anthony Appiah, who argues:
I think about [Johann Gottfried] Herder whenever people argue that Italian or Malian or Chinese artworks should "go home," because the idea that art belongs to nations is one of his more unfortunate legacies. Art from everywhere can matter to people from anywhere. Those of us who live in the city of the Metropolitan Museum know that extremely well. So though I can think of lots of good reasons for repatriating art—that it was stolen, that it's site-specific, that there isn't a lot of art of its kind in the place it's going back to—the idea that art belongs in a national home is not among them.

Anthony Appiah, "There Is No National Home for Art," *New York Times*, January 22, 2015. Nevertheless, many nations restrict the export of what they regard as their national treasures. See, e.g., Francesco Francioni and Ana Filipa Vrdoljak, eds., *The Oxford Handbook of International Cultural Heritage Law* (Oxford, UK: Oxford University Press, 2020); and Treasure Act 1996, UK Public General Acts 1996, Chapter 24.

15 Critics of NAGPRA point to the vagueness of its terms. For example, cultural patrimony is defined as "an object having ongoing historical, traditional, or cultural importance central to the Native American group or culture itself, rather than property owned by an individual Native American, and which, therefore, cannot be alienated, appropriated, or conveyed by any individual regardless of whether or not the individual is a member of the Indian tribe." The Biden administration's Department of the Interior, in recommending changes to NAGPRA, has stated that one goal is to "[s]treamline existing regulatory requirements by eliminating ambiguities, correcting inaccuracies, simplifying excessively burdensome and complicated requirements, clarifying timelines and removing offensive terminology in the existing regulations." Zachary Small, "Push to Return 116,000 Native American Remains is Long-Awaited," *New York Times*, August 6, 2021.

16 Statutes providing for land purchases include the Land Buy Back Program for Tribal Nations (purchase of fractionated shares, pursuant to *Cobell v. Salazar*, 679 F.3d 909 (D.C. Cir. 2012)); and Claims Resolution Act of 2010, 42 U.S.C. § 1305. In a number of instances Native Americans have bought back property on the open market. See Colin Woodard, "Passamaquoddy Tribe Reacquires Island Stolen Nearly 160 Years Ago," *Portland* (Maine) *Press Herald*, May 20, 2021. For the case that land should be included as cultural property, see Lindsey L. Wiersma, "Note, Indigenous Lands as Cultural Property: A New Approach to Indigenous Land Claims," *Duke Law Journal* 54 (2005): 1061–88.

17 Virginia Woolf, *A Room of One's Own* (1957) [1929]. See also *Bulun Bulan v. R & T Textiles Pty Ltd.* (Federal Court of Australia 1998), 157 A. L. R. 193 (native artist has fiduciary duty to his community for copyrighted work he based on tribal designs). On the movement by museums to attribute native works of art to individual artists, see Judith H. Dobrzynski, "Honoring Art, Honoring Artists," *New York Times*, February 6, 2011. California's *droit de suite* statute was upheld only for in-state transactions. See *Sam Francis Foundation v. Christie's Inc.*, 784 F.3d 1320 (9th Cir. 2015).

18 In addition to the *Chilkat* case cited above at note 11, see, e.g., Miranda Forsyth, "Lifting the Lid on 'The Community': Who Has the Right to Control Access to Traditional Knowledge and Expressions of Culture?" *International Journal of Cultural Property* 19, no. 1 (2012): 1–31.

19 Preference may be given tribes in such areas as hiring or marketing. See, e.g., *Morton v. Mancari*, 417 U.S. 535, 554 (1974) ("The preference, as applied, is granted to Indians not as a discrete racial group, but rather, as members of quasi-sovereign tribal entities whose lives and activities are governed by the BIA

[Bureau of Indian Affairs] in a unique fashion."). See also Indian Arts and Crafts Act, 104 Stat. 4664 (1990) (specifying penalties for faking Indian handcrafted goods), and William J. Hapiuk, Jr., "Of Kitsch and Kachinas: A Critical Analysis of the Indian Arts and Crafts Act of 1990," *Stanford Law Review* 53, no. 4 (2001): 1009–75.

7. THE SHORTAGE IS NOT ONLY OF WATER

1 See generally Erum Sattar, Jason Robison, and Daniel McCool, "Evolution of Water Institutions in the Indus River Basin: Reflections from the Law of the Colorado River," *University of Michigan Journal of Law Reform* 51, no. 4 (2018): 715–75, https://repository.law.umich.edu/mjlr/vol51/iss4/3; David Owen, "The Biggest Potential Water Disaster in the United States," *The New Yorker*, May 11, 2022; and Karin Brulliard, "The Colorado River Is in Crisis, and It's Getting Worse Every Day," *Washington Post*, May 14, 2022.

2 For the Morocco-Spain connection, see the following works by Thomas F. Glick: *Irrigation and Society in Medieval Valencia* (Cambridge, MA: Harvard University Press, 1970); *The Old World Background of the Irrigation System of San Antonio, Texas*, Southwestern Studies Monograph No. 35 (San Antonio: Texas Western Press, 1972), 3–67; *From Muslim Fortress to Christian Castle: Social and Cultural Change in Medieval Spain* (Manchester, UK: Manchester University Press, 1995), 69–76; and "Hydraulic Technology in al-Andalus," in Salma Khadra Jayyusi, ed., *The Legacy of Muslim Spain*, vol. 2 (Leiden: E. J. Brill, 1992), 974–86. For the Mexican-California connection, see Mark Kanazawa, *Golden Rules: The Origins of California Water Law in the Gold Rush* (Chicago: University of Chicago Press, 2015); and John B. Clayberg, "The Genesis and Development of the Law of Waters in the Far West," *Michigan Law Review* 1, no. 2 (November 1902): 91–101. On the legal recognition of miners' customary water law, see *Irwin v. Phillips*, 5 Cal. 140 (1855). See generally Ray Huffaker, Norman Whittlesey, and Joel R. Hamilton, "The Role of Prior Appropriation in Allocating Water Resources Into the 21st Century," *International Journal of Water Resources Development* 16, no. 2 (2000): 265–73; and Judith Scheele, "Rightful Measures: Irrigation, Land, and the Shari'ah in the Algerian Touat," in Paul Dresch and Hannah Skoda, eds., *Legalism: Anthropology and History* (Oxford, UK: University Press, 2012), 197–228.

3 As noted by Yossef Rapoport and Ido Shahar, "Irrigation in Medieval Islamic Fayyum: Local Control in a Large Scale Hydraulic System," *Journal of the Economic and Social History of the Orient* 55, no. 1 (2012):1–31, 6: "[A] dominant theme of the study of rural society in mediaeval al-Andalus has been the predominance of local control. Thomas Glick, building on previous studies by Barcelo, Guichard, and Bazzana, argues that, in almost all irrigation systems, except for the large-scale macro-systems, tribal organization has been particularly suitable for managing rights to water and resolving conflicts between upstream and downstream communities."

4   Clifford Geertz, "The Wet and the Dry: Traditional Irrigation in Bali and Mo-
    rocco," *Human Ecology* 1, no. 1 (March 1972): 23–39, 37.

5   This feature is underscored by the treatment of subsurface water rights as an even
    more intensively private ownership regime in the American West. See gener-
    ally Gerald Torres, "Liquid Assets: Groundwater in Texas," *Yale Law Journal
    Online*, no. 122 (2012): 143–66, https://papers.ssrn.com/sol3/papers.cfm?abstract_
    id=2188690. On the scandal concerning Saudi Arabia's control of groundwater
    in Arizona, see Natalie Koch, *Arid Empire: The Entangled Fates of Arizona and
    Arabia* (London: Verso, 2023), and Natalie Koch, "Arizona Is in a Race to the Bot-
    tom of Its Water Wells, With Saudi Arabia's Help," *New York Times*, December 26,
    2022.

6   Alexis de Tocqueville, *Democracy in America*, vol 2, trans. Harvey C. Mansfield
    and Delba Winthrop (Chicago: University of Chicago Press, 2000), 482.

7   The contrast to Greek science, for example, is notable: "Even so, there is some
    foundation for the traditional story—as old as Aristotle—that speculation about
    nature was revolutionised by a group of Greeks from the sixth century BC
    onwards. . . . As far as we can tell, there was no instrumental reason for these
    [naturalistic] intellectual endeavours: they were conducted for their own sake,
    or because a life of contemplation was considered a life well spent. . . . The aims
    of Islamic science were less abstract and more instrumental than the Greeks' had
    been." Dmitri Levitin, "Such Matters as the Soul," *London Review of Books* 38, no.
    18 (September 22, 2016): 29–32.

8   On the current viability of the prior appropriation system, see Reed D. Benson,
    "Alive But Irrelevant: The Prior Appropriation Doctrine in Today's Western Water
    Law," *University of Colorado Law Review* 83, no. 3 (2012): 676–714. On the acequia
    system, see Stanley Crawford, *Mayordomo: Chronicle of an Acequia in Northern
    New Mexico* (Albuquerque: University of New Mexico Press, 1993); Gregory A.
    Hicks and Devon G. Peña, "Community *Acequias* in Colorado's Rio Culebra
    Watershed: A Customary Commons in the Domain of Prior Appropriation,"
    University of Colorado Law Review 74, no. 2 (2003): 387–486; Michael Cox and
    Justin M. Ross, "Robustness and Vulnerability of Community Irrigation Systems:
    The Case of the Taos Valley Acequias," *Journal of Environmental Economics and
    Management* 61, no. 3 (May 2011): 254–66; and Roberto Lovato, "Acequias and
    the Hydraulic Genius of Shari'ah Law," *Craftsmanship Quarterly* (Summer 2022
    [Winter 2017]), https://craftsmanship.net/the-hydraulic-genius-of-shariah-law.

9   Each almond requires approximately 3.2 gallons of water. Put differently, one acre
    of mature almond trees requires roughly 1.3 million gallons of water per year. In
    California, almonds use up 10 percent of available water, the alfalfa used for cattle
    feed 15 percent. For more specifics, see Julian Fulton, Michael Norton, and Fraser
    Shilling, "Water-Indexed Benefits and Impacts of California Almonds," *Ecologi-
    cal Indicators* 96, part 1 (January 2019): 711–17. It also takes more than thirty-eight
    gallons of water to produce a quarter-pound of beef. See J. Poore and T. Nemecek,
    "Reducing Food's Environmental Impacts through Producers and Consum-

ers," *Science* 360, no. 6392 (2018): 987–92. See also Brian D. Richter et al., "Water Scarcity and Fish Imperilment Driven by Beef Production," *Nature Sustainability* 3 (2020): 319–28.

10 *Kelo v. City of New London*, 545 U.S. 469 (2005).

11 For an extended discussion of trust in the Arab world, see Lawrence Rosen, *The Justice of Islam* (Oxford, UK: Oxford University Press, 2000), 133–50.

12 Fran Korten, "The Science of Cooperation," *UTNE Reader*, August 5, 2010, www.utne.com/politics/science-cooperation-commons-elinor-ostrom. Ostrom, who wrote her doctoral dissertation on groundwater management in California, is perhaps best known for her book *Governing the Commons: The Evolution of Institutions for Collective Action* (Cambridge UK: Cambridge University Press, 1990). For a relevant view of flexible rules, see Lorraine Daston, *Rules: A Short History of What We Live By* (Princeton, NJ: Princeton University Press, 2022).

13 See Stephen N. Bretsen and Peter J. Hill, "Irrigation Institutions in the American West," *UCLA Journal of Environmental Law and Policy* 25 (2006–2007): 283–331.

14 The special role of Native American water rights is vital to any such consideration. For background on the situation in the Colorado River Basin and Indian water rights, see Matthew McKinney, Jay Weiner, and Daryl Vigil, "First in Time: The Place of Tribes in Governing the Colorado River System," *Natural Resources Journal* 63, no. 2 (2023): 283–313. On the important role women can play in native water rights, see Heather Tanana, "Voices of the River: The Rise of Indigenous Women Leaders in the Colorado River Basin," *Colorado Environmental Law Journal* 34, no. 2 (2023) 265–98.

8. THE PRUDENT INVESTOR RULE AND THE DUTY TO COMMUNITY

1 *Harvard College v. Amory*, 26 Mass (9 Pick), 446, 448 (1830).

2 For long-term data on changes in endowment market value (which is not the same as rates of return), see www.nacubo.org/Research/2021/Historic-Endowment-Study-Data.

3 Stephanie Mitchell, "Q and A on Harvard's Financial Report," *Harvard Gazette*, October 16, 2009.

4 Juliet Chung and Melissa Korn, "After Record Year, University-Endowment Returns Drop Into Negative Territory," *Wall Street Journal*, October 21, 2022.

5 See B. T., "A Down Year," *Princeton Alumni Weekly*, December 2022, 8.

6 Michael T. Nietzel, "Stanford and Yale Endowment Returns Are Up, While MIT and Duke See Losses Again," *Forbes*, October 13, 2023, www.forbes.com/sites/michaeltnietzel/2023/10/13/stanford-and-yale-endowment-returns-are-up-while-mit-and-duke-see-losses-again/?sh=456296107192.

7 See Hamza Shaban and Rachel Lerman, "These Tech Moguls Lost a Combined $433 Billion This Year," *Washington Post*, December 27, 2022.

8 For examples of the price paid by employees, students, and others in 2008–2009 period, see James J. Fishman, "What Went Wrong: Prudent Management of En-

dowment Funds and Imprudent Endowment Investing Policies," *Journal of College & University Law* 40, no. 2 (2014): 199–244, app. I, 241–46.

9 *Harvard College v. Amory*, 26 Mass (9 Pick) 446 (1830). On the historical background to the prudent investor rule, see Mayo Adams Shattuck, "The Development of the Prudent Man Rule for Fiduciary Investment in the United States in the Twentieth Century," *Ohio State Law Journal* 12, no. 4 (1951): 491–521.

10 See www.investopedia.com/terms/u/uniform-prudent-investor-act.asp. The rule was superseded without significant change by Restatement (Third) of Trusts § 90 (Minneapolis: American Law Institute, 2007). For an interesting application of the prior rule and the use of an advisory jury in its adjudication, see *First Alabama Bank of Montgomery, NA v. Martin*, 425 So. 2d 415 (Alabama Supreme Court 1982). For a summary analysis of cases under the prior rule, see Paul G. Haskell, "The Prudent Person Rule for Trustee Investment and the Modern Portfolio Theory," *North Carolina Law Review* 69, no. 1 (1990): 87–111, 94–99.

11 For a dissenting view on the new prudent investor rule's encouragement of modern portfolio theory, see Haskell, "The Prudent Person Rule," 108–11. On modern portfolio theory, see *id.*, 100–08. The courts have ruled that anyone investing funds for a trust must remove imprudent investments in a timely fashion. See *Hughes v. Northwestern University*, 142 S. Ct. 737 (2022), and *Tibble v. Edison Int'l.*, 575 U.S. 523 (2015).

12 On the relation of the rule to investments like the S&P 500 and derivatives, see Robert J. Aalberts and Percy S. Poon, "Derivatives and the Modern Prudent Investor Rule: Too Risky or Too Necessary?" *Ohio State Law Journal* 67, no. 3 (2006), 525–92. See also *Thole v. U.S. Bank N. A.*, 140 S. Ct. 1615 (2020) (Sotomayor, J., dissenting).

13 For additional examples, see Josh Moody, "Endowment Returns Fall," *Inside Higher Education*, November 8, 2022, www.insidehighered.com/news/2022/11/08/endowment-returns-drop-across-higher-education.

14 For examples of unwise revenue devices employed by some public school systems, see Gretchen Morgenson, "Exotic Deals Put Denver Schools Deeper in Debt," *New York Times*, August 5, 2010.

15 See generally John H. Langbein, "The Uniform Prudent Investor Act and the Future of Trust Investing," *Iowa Law Review* 81 (1996): 641–69.

16 Stewart E. Sterk, "Rethinking Trust Law Reform: How Prudent Is Modern Prudent Investor Doctrine?" *Cornell Law Review* 95, no. 5 (2010): 851–904.

17 Max M. Schanzenbach and Robert H. Sitkoff, "The Prudent Investor Rule and Market Risk: An Empirical Analysis," *Journal of Empirical Legal Studies* 14, no. 1 (March 2017): 129–68.

18 For an earlier study based on a survey of institutional investors, see Martin D. Begleiter, "Does the Prudent Investor Need the Uniform Prudent Investor Act—An Empirical Study of Trust Investment Practices," *Maine Law Review* 51, no. 1 (1999): 27–85.

19 Gutman later received a record deferred payout of $23 million. James H. Finkelstein and Judith A. Wilde, "A Shady, Secret Presidential Perk," *Chronicle of Higher Education*, September 11, 2023.

20 John Gray, "We Simply Do Not Know," *London Review of Books* 31, no. 22 (November 19, 2009).

21 John Cassidy, *How Markets Fail: The Logic of Economic Calamities* (New York: Farrar, Straus and Giroux, 2009). See also Fishman, "What Went Wrong."

22 Beth Healy, "Ex-Employee Says She Warned Harvard of Risky Moves: Endowment Staffer Fired After Letter to President," *Boston Globe*, April 3, 2009.

23 Fishman, "What Went Wrong,"201.

24 See generally Michael N. Bastedo, "Conflicts, Commitments, and Cliques in the University: Moral Seduction as a Threat to Trustee Independence," *American Educational Research Journal* 46, no. 2 (2009): 354–86.

25 See *Thole v. US Bank N. A.* (Sotomayor, J., dissenting), text and citations at note 6.

26 Considerations other than those of economic maximization are difficult to reconcile with the current prudent investor structure. As Langbein (in "The Uniform Prudent Investor Act," 643) notes: "[E]ven though the Uniform Prudent Investor Act is default law that the settlor of the trust can alter or oust, the Act is likely to limit the settlor's power to impose manifestly uneconomic investment restrictions." One man's "uneconomic restrictions" may, of course, be another man's principled goals (e.g., not investing in booming fossil fuel industries but in lower-yielding "green" projects). For the argument that universities should not, however, mix investing strategies with social policy, see John H. Langbein and Richard A. Posner, "Social Investing and the Law of Trusts," *Michigan Law Review* 79, no. 1 (1980): 72–112, 111–12. ("Charitable trusts have been designed to serve specialized purposes—in education, healing, the arts, research, and so forth. They are not well suited to be fora for the resolution of complex social issues largely unrelated to their work. There is every reason to think that charitable trustees will best serve the cause of social change by remitting the advocates of various social causes to the political arena, where their proposals can be fairly tested and defined, and if found meritorious, effectively implemented.") The idea that an organization must wait until the federal government sets policies that guide how the organization may invest its own monies is to grant both the government and the invisible hand of the market a control many would find insupportable. For further examples of trustee risk-taking and disagreements over social investing, along with suggestions for reform, see L. Robert Guenthner, Kathleen Nilles, and Sheldon E. Steinbach, "Investment Policies Are Not Optional," *Chronicle of Higher Education* 51, no. 48 (August 5, 2005) (section titled "Endowments," B24).

INDEX

abortion 21, 33–34, 37, 48–54
alternative dispute resolution 60, 62

Bellah, Robert 4
Blackmun, Harry (Justice), 37–39, 51
blasphemy laws, 56
Bork, Robert (Judge), 41
Burger, Warren (Chief Justice), 60
burials, Native American, 69–89; and
    ancient remains, 71; and proposed
    legislation, 87–89; numbers of remains,
    72; practices, 70

Catholics, on Supreme Court, 40–42
community, American romance of, 1; and
    law, 13; concept of, 4, 115
conscience, concept of in the law, 23–25
cultural property, proposed legisla-
    tion, 95–99. *See also* indigenous
    peoples
culture, concept of, 6–9, 11–12, 29–30
custom, legal concept of, 25–28; and legal
    history, 26–27

Dart, Raymond, 5–6
defamation, group, 14, 55–65; other na-
    tions' laws on, 57; proposed legislation,
    63–65
dignity, legal concept of, 52–53
diversity, legal concept of, 51–54
DNA testing, 69, 71, 73, 79, 83–84, 86
doubt, legal expressions of, 34–47

expert witnesses, 86

Frankfurter, Felix (Justice), 20–21, 23–25,
    33

Hand, Learned (Judge), 34
Hart, H.L.A., 35, 60, 75–76

Indian Claims Commission, 61, 76–77, 88
indigenous peoples, 14; and access to
    sacred sites, 94; courts of, 79; valuation
    of cultural property, 90–99

Jewish Conciliation Board, 61–62, 78–79,
    88
John Paul II (Pope), encyclical by, 41
judicial restraint, 45–46
juries, 64, 74

law, uses of history in, 22

Native American Graves Protection Act
    (NAGPRA), 71; and specialized court
    proposal, 73–76
Ninth Amendment, 14, 49, 51–52

Marshall, John (Chief Justice), 72
multiplex relations, 29–30

Ostrom, Elinor, 105–106

Posner, Richard (Judge), 90–91, 124n21
prudent investor rule, 107–14

Rawls, John, 84
Raz, Joseph, 82–83

Reisman, David, 4
Roberts, John (Chief Justice), 34, 43

Scalia, Antonin (Justice), 41, 122n22

Tocqueville, Alexis de, 2–4, 103
"traditions of our people" 13, 19–23, 116, 123n6
tribes, 92

truth and conciliation, 62–63

uncertainty, in law, 33–47

Waldron, Jeremy, 83–84
Walzer, Michael, 83
water rights, and irrigation, 100–106; and
    Western water law, 102–3

ABOUT THE AUTHOR

LAWRENCE ROSEN is the William Nelson Cromwell Professor of Anthropology Emeritus at Princeton University and Adjunct Professor Emeritus of Law at Columbia University. Named to the first group of MacArthur Award recipients, he has authored more than a dozen books, including *Law as Culture*, *The Justice of Islam*, and *Legitimacy in Crisis*.

www.ingramcontent.com/pod-product-compliance
Lightning Source LLC
Chambersburg PA
CBHW031534260326
41914CB00032B/1803/J